OF ONE
HEART

LOOK BACK
AT SODOM

Deseret Book Company
Salt Lake City, Utah

This book is not an official Church publication;
the author is solely responsible for the content.

First printing in combined edition, October 1990

ISBN 0-87579-420-3

Printed in the United States of America

10   9   8   7   6   5   4   3   2   1

Publisher's Preface

Although scripture provides scant information about the ancient cities of Sodom and Enoch, those accounts nevertheless convey a poignant message of the sorrow of sin and the joy of righteousness. What scripture teaches about the moral depravity and consequent destruction of Sodom can be as powerful a motivator to righteousness as the accounts of Enoch's ministry and the glory of his Zion.

Elder Neal A. Maxwell's books *Look Back at Sodom* and *Of One Heart* address that very purpose. Based on scripture, the writings of latter-day prophets, and the best secular sources, his fictionalized accounts of what life might have been like during those times are powerful reminders of the parallels, both bleak and glorious, between the fates of those cities and the directions taken by modern society and us as individuals.

In counterpointing the cataclysm of Sodom with the glory of the city of Enoch, Elder Maxwell offers an intriguing perspective on the timeless theme of striving for perfection in an imperfect world.

OF ONE HEART

The Glory
of the
City of Enoch

To Enoch,

whose faith moved not only mountains, but, more importantly, men; and to his successful people for showing us that it can be done: that lapsed righteousness is not inevitable and that near-celestial culture can be transmitted from generation to generation; and with anticipation of that remarkable rendezvous when this prophet and his people return.

> *And the Lord said unto Enoch: Then shalt thou and all thy city meet them there, and we will receive them into our bosom, and they shall see us; and we will fall upon their necks, and they shall fall upon our necks, and we will kiss each other;*
>
> *And there shall be mine abode, and it shall be Zion, which shall come forth out of all the creations which I have made; and for the space of a thousand years the earth shall rest. (Moses 7:63–64.)*

3

INTRODUCTION

Just as the disappearance of Sodom and its sister cities was unprecedented, so was the translation—or removal heaven-ward[1]—of the city of Enoch centuries before Sodom. The Old and New Testaments (from Genesis to Jude) and, more generously, modern scriptures confirm the existence of the city of Enoch.

A confluence of conditions and characteristics led to the disintegration of Sodom, for Sodom was not just a place, but a way of life. A confluence of sharply different conditions and characteristics created the sublime city-culture of Enoch.

Countless secular and sectarian utopian schemes have been stillborn or have soon gone awry, but, significantly, a sustained Christ-centered society did exist, and it is a true story that cries out to be told.

There are several relevant reasons for attempting to ponder probingly the city of Enoch. First, in our time of increasing perplexity among nations and individual despair, it is important to realize that thousands of people ages ago successfully applied the commandments of God and thereby had great and unparalleled happiness. Sec-

---

[1]Translation is not a literal resurrection, but a specific change whereby those selected do not "taste of death." Later they will be changed in a "twinkling of an eye" from mortality to immortality. (3 Nephi 28.)

ond, since God sets both incentives and warnings before mankind, it is just as important to have before us the positive consequences of righteousness as well as the negative consequences of sin. Third, God preserved and prepared Enoch's people in the midst of awful and enveloping evil, and, reassuringly, he has promised his people in our own time that though "great tribulations shall be among the children of men, . . . my people will I preserve." (Moses 7:61.) The Lord has also said that the day will come "when peace shall be taken from the earth, and the devil shall have power over his dominion. And also the Lord shall have power over his saints, and shall reign in their midst. . . . " (D&C 1:35–36.) Fourth, the pending rendezvous between the people of Enoch's city-culture and those to be preserved on the earth at the time of Christ's second coming will be utterly unique in all of human history and is worthy of some quiet anticipation.

First, it was Enoch alone — except for his heavenly helpers. Then a handful of humans joined him. Soon there was a colony. Then a city!

There appear to be no new or complex doctrines that would account for the unique outcome in the city of Enoch. One will look in vain in the scriptures for a single spectacular teaching that accounts for this singular and spectacular event. Clearly, what made these people unique was their serious and steady application of the simple teachings of Jesus Christ. That is the great message that this book aims at underscoring.

The device chosen — *imaginary communications* from Mahijah (Moses 6:40) to his imaginary friend Omner — permits some literary flexibility.[2] The basic information

---

[2]The author is assuming, happily, that when the real Mahijah questioned Enoch, it was not a casual question nor an effort to entrap. The question might have sprung from Mahijah's desire to know more about Enoch. If so, Mahijah's soul would have quickened at the response, a foreshadowing of his being drawn even closer to Enoch.

about this remarkable city-culture is derived from scriptures, ancient and modern. Selected statements by modern Church leaders about the city of Enoch are found in Appendix B.

Quotation marks that would normally entwine excerpts from scriptures emerging after Enoch's time are omitted to ease the passage of the eye and to blend with the intimate conversational tone intended.

The literary register of these communications is unlike the style used in the companion booklet, *Look Back at Sodom.* This book assumes too that only some of Mahijah's *imaginary communications* (sent from inside the city of Enoch to Omner on the outside) survived, giving us only a glimpse of the gradual glory that came to the city of Enoch. There is one unexplained but lengthy gap of many years when Omner does not appear to encourage Mahijah's further communications.

The author assumes that all but one of Omner's communications to Mahijah stayed with Mahijah and were thus lost to this world, though Mahijah makes reference to some of Omner's concerns and comments.[3]

While the author has tried diligently not to go beyond what we find about the city of Enoch in scriptures or in the utterances of modern prophets, imaginary communications, of necessity, create the possibility of misunderstanding unless the reader is prayerful, careful, and discerning.

The reader may also need some fresh familiarity with the actual scriptures about the city of Enoch. *For this purpose the serious reader should read, or reread, chapters 6, 7, and 8 of Moses before reading this booklet.* (A synopsis of these chapters is provided in Appendix A.)

Also, since Enoch and his people were good enough

---

[3]The lone exception, a letter from Omner, was never finished nor sent for reasons shown later.

to be translated, the author assumes they were at least as good as were the Nephites of A.D. 36–111. Therefore, the Nephites' positive characteristics and traits as described in Fourth Nephi are woven into this account. (A synopsis of that book is in Appendix C.)

Finally, since the residue of the inhabitants of the earth in Enoch's time were regarded by God as the most wicked among all his creations, the author assumes those outside the city of Enoch were at least as bad as were the Nephites of A.D. 400–421. (See Moroni 9.) Therefore, use is also made of comparative negative characteristics and traits in certain of the *imaginary communications*.

My Honored Friend Omner, Greetings!

Since seeing you last, I have thought often of how much I cherish our conversations. I know of your restless desire to be ever apprised of the latest happenings, but first, my friend, I hope this epistle finds all well in the land of Omner and that your crops progress toward a bounteous harvest.

I advise you now of the presence in my city of a strange and wild man by the name of Enoch. It is because of your fascination with the philosophies and sayings of men that I speak of this man Enoch. I do not expect he will become a man of even local importance. Even so, his first advent amongst us was unsettling.

Enoch is apparently a son of Jared, whose people are said to be hard-working and harmless. Yet he caused unease and fear among some here who heard him, even though he is young and noticeably slow of speech.

All who heard him, and I, too, were offended in one manner or another. It was his certitude, in particular, that troubled me. Indeed, I was one of the few who chose to confront him, asking him to tell us plainly who he was and whence he came. He gave a straightforward answer, but then riled us all by saying that while he had been journeying from the land of Cainan by the sea east, he had received a vision. He even made bold to say the Lord had commanded him to come forth and preach to us. He spoke at length, detaining many of us from our appointed rounds by reason of our curiosity.

I have it in mind to hear Enoch again tomorrow, for he is roving over the countryside speaking on the hills and high places, or wherever he can find people willing to endure his testifying. How does he expect to gain much of a following? He is so filled with alarms and denunciation, and he disturbs the even flow of life here.

Since he gave me more than a passing glance as I challenged him about his origins, I felt he was challenging me to dare to be again among his listeners. I shall not disappoint him, though he is hardly worth the effort.

Enoch spoke of certain records coming down to us through outstanding patriarchs going back to Adam. I can scarcely believe such records mean much to our time, having been written by men much advanced in years — hardly a reliable guide for those of us confronted with the snares and entanglements of a later time. Have you heard of such records? If so, Omner, what doctrines are contained therein? Enoch says we have neglected these teachings.

Please write to me, for your words would console me in the distance that life now places between us.

Your father, after whom your land of Omner is named, might not be pleased to know that this land, along with others, has been called upon by Enoch to repent. I trust you will send that warning around speedily, Omner, lest your people be smitten with a curse and die. But before you take care of that exacting task, please send me any news you may have. Accept again my gratitude for the gift of that splendid ruby, for it is my joy and treasure.

Yours with all respect,
Mahijah

Greetings to My Honored Friend Omner!

I write even before receiving your response to my previous epistle to heighten your interest in the pilgrim now among us, this man Enoch. I confess that at first I found him amusing and comical; now I wonder if he will not obtain something of a following. The leaders of the people are beginning to be vexed by him. How can he assume to denounce our way of life and win our support? Does he not know that to get along here he must go along with things as they are?

Enoch received coincidental help the other day when the earth shook at the very time he was making one of his speeches. The tremor prevented some who would clearly have laid hold upon him from doing so, because they were unable to remain standing. Strangely enough, he seemed not to be affected by the tremors and rumblings. I fully expect him to be apprehended soon, for he can hardly expect the earth always to tremble so conveniently.

It would be so good if you were here to converse about the eccentricities of this ecclesiastic, Enoch. Come as soon as your affairs will permit, that we may sup and converse about this and all matters of state. Your wit and wisdom are much needed.

Have you word of any newly arrived precious stones I might buy, or are you yet ready to sell me your own prize ruby? You know of my greed for good gems!

One matter for you to ponder: if this man Enoch has lived among an apparently pleasant people in the land of his father, why would he leave such a life to risk the growing hostility of the crowds in my city? You may reply that he is merely a man who searches for satisfactions and recognitions that could not be obtained in his pastoral homeland. It is a teasing question, is it not, for Enoch is clearly astute enough to know that each day he is here, he is risking his life.

I remain your devoted colleague,
Mahijah

My Honorable and Wise Omner,
Greetings and Salutations!

I am indebted, after these many months, for your lengthy epistle. I immediately ceased what I was doing to reflect upon its contents.

You are more intrigued by this man Enoch than I expected. I was startled that you assume the existence of the patriarchal records to which he referred. Have you actually seen them? In any event, he now seems to have turned the more part of the people against him, because of the sting of his sayings.

You asked for my assessment of the man. Having now heard him four times, I have concluded that he is no fool. His straightforwardness, while it counters so many of the traditions in our time, is refreshing. He denounces the devised murders that some in this city have used to keep their place in power. You know of my contempt for those who must resort to violence when their words fall, unpersuasively, to the ground.

I have been wrong about Enoch in one matter: no one has laid hands upon him yet, and I am not certain that they will now. There was a time when this was possible, and I so told you. He seems too skillful and too well established to be vulnerable to interference with his preachings. While it was earth tremors that first deterred his detractors, now there is a hesitancy among his enemies that seems to be rooted in fear of him.

Yet there is a gentleness about him, even a mildness and meekness in his bold denunciations. He truly sees himself as being on an errand for the Lord, whom he calls our Savior to come.

Yesterday in one of his sermons he prophesied the fates of various nations. He omitted no one, and his predictions are dire. The future is dreadful, if we were to believe this stranger in our land.

Behold, my servants inform me that Enoch is but a few short rods away from my house, even now. I go now to gain fresh word for you about this pilgrim. It gives me a special sense of excitement to be able to do so at the very time I am writing you.

Some hours have passed, Omner, but more may have transpired than the mere passage of time. I have now heard Enoch discuss what he calls God's "plan of salvation" for mankind, without which Enoch says we are all lost. It is the most daring and simple explanation of life I have ever heard, though it was consistent with itself.

You and I have talked about the philosophies of men many times, observing how the philosophies of men seem to have no fixed reference points. Not so with Enoch. He perceives truth, and something called priesthood, as coming down to us in a straight line from Adam through patriarchs, some of whom live still. You can see why his views caused a stir here in my city, where so many spend their time in nothing else but either to tell or to hear some new thing.

You know from our sharings in the past that while I have not been religious, I am not one of those who believe that life is explainable without acknowledging the existence of a God, though I have resisted the efforts of factions to capture God as if he were their own private trophy. Enoch does not give me that tribal feeling.

Men seem to me to belong to such factions solely to increase the strength of their own voices, to give them the courage they otherwise lack, or to get gain by multiplying their power. The unselfish, like you, Omner, look outward upon their fellowman with consideration as to how they might serve them, but those in the fellowship of factions are self-serving. Enoch says the forces of evil are led by the father of factions, Satan, who pretends that he is the only begotten of God, the Father.

service vs. selfishness

13

You see how this Enoch is no ordinary itinerant?

I must confess I stayed to the end of what he had to say. He seemed to remember me from the time when I first asked him the question. Along with a few others, I also remained afterwards in informal conversation with him. It gave me a chance to ask him several questions without the cacophony of the crowd about us.

I wish you could meet this man, Omner!

A tent-keeper from the hills, who likewise remained after, told me that in his strong desire to hear Enoch, he had hastily told others to keep his tents so that he could come "to behold the seer."

Many have hearkened to Enoch, but the common people seem to hear him most gladly. He seeks to bring all men to God, saying, "He is my God, and your God." He not only calls all men his brethren, but actually treats all in that manner. He opens his mouth, and it is filled with warm words of wisdom.

Omner, I feel the need of your friendship now more than ever, for there are strange stirrings within me. Perhaps it is more from a mixture of fatigue and excitement than the power of Enoch.

You and I have a pact under which we always tell each other the truth. That pact now requires me to say that I can no longer take Enoch lightly. I must hear even more from him in order that I may dispose of this whole matter.

His sayings are not incoherent babblings; he is a person of consequence. Though I previously complained of his slowness of speech, I now find the content of what he says so compelling that I scarcely notice his speech.

Please do not be alarmed; I am not yet about to yield to his teachings, but neither am I any longer in a position to dismiss his doctrines. There is a boldness about them, and one must dismiss all of them or none of them. Once you accept his assumption, then his logic carries you over a threshold you might prefer not to cross. His assumptions

14

can be rejected, but he has a way of coming back to these principles that is both forceful and exciting.

Please be as candid with me, my friend, as I have been with you. I count on your candor as well as your concern.

One final observation. In one of your epistles, Omner, you mentioned your view that as humans we are individually accountable for the mistakes we make, being slow to lay blame on our ancestors for acts we ourselves commit. That is the fearful thing that Enoch says! He views man as knowing sufficiently to distinguish good from evil and as being truly free to obey or disobey the laws of God. It is a searching approach in an age when so many among us are willing to forget our ancestors in consequence of our concern over our present predicaments. Indeed, Enoch seems at one with his ancestors and speaks warmly and personally of them. Clearly, his heart is much turned to his fathers.

What is in the memory and mind truly controls our conduct. To be sure, there are times when men would do evil, but only circumstances prevent it. Recall, Omner, the aging thief we watched years ago in the marketplace trying to steal a nobleman's coin purse. There was larceny in his heart but his legs were honest, you wittily observed, as the limping thief was overtaken!

Your friend,
Mahijah

To My Dear but Preoccupied Friend Omner:

My discontent deepened to learn, upon my return after many weeks, that there was no missive from you, though my servants advised me that they themselves placed in your very hands my last epistle to you. I had hoped otherwise. I looked forward, more than you know, for a response from you, for I shall now be gone again for some time, having concluded that I will accompany Enoch even farther in his journeys.

I leave things in my own household somewhat unsettled too, for there are those here who are much troubled and exercised that I have found fascination, not fault, with the words of Enoch. Surely several messages from you will await me then, preferably your presence. Yet I know of your heavy responsibilities in the affairs of men.

By now I have had much time to associate with the followers of Enoch, who, incidentally, are speaking of forming a little colony that they think one day might become a city. I am not sanguine — but Enoch's followers are not long-faced and sad; they are a happy and smiling people who pay much heed to the needs of each other. Their striking individuality seems to be heightened, not lessened, by their faith in Jesus Christ, who, they say, is the ultimate Redeemer to come. Their unity is not the conformity that you and I have seen imposed by the sword; it rests upon mutual esteem and mutual desires. Such consequences count for much with me.

Omner, you once said of the afflicted who are all about us that you and I are not responsible for their condition. If you mean their lameness or blindness, then what you spoke is true. Yet if my experience amongst the Enochians is any guide, you and I are accountable for their present conditions of life; if by withholding fellowship we fail to sweeten their lot, we have added to their affliction. I quake at such duties to my fellowmen as Enoch sets forth; he does not say such duties are easy, but that such are imperative.

Where some leaders flatter their followers, thus diminishing their sense of duty, Enoch flatters his followers in yet a different way. He believes in his people not only for what they are, but for what they have the power to become.

Enoch is more than simply a strong leader. He is a

16

leader who leads out of love. His is a desire to serve people, not to be elevated and enthroned by them. He is a simple, yet wise, man. His followers give me hope by continuing to teach me that others may know, just as he knows, about the surety of what he preaches. Already his people seem set apart from the rest of the citizens in this city.

Some say that Enoch is more than a prophet—that he is a seer. There was a time, I am told, when he was concerned that the people hated him, wondering why the Lord would select to do his work a person who is despised. Those close to Enoch say, however, that the Lord sees not as man sees, for man looks on the outward appearance, but the Lord looks on the heart, and thus Enoch became his emissary.

I must say that I am now beyond the point of feeling the need to question Enoch and those about him. He speaks with power of the experience he had when he went up on Mount Simeon. While upon the mount, he says, the heavens opened and he saw the Lord, who revealed the prospects of various peoples and nations. He was given a commandment that he should baptize in the name of the Father and the Son and the Holy Ghost. In that simple step, about which I shall write more later, we can measure the piercing thrust of Enoch's ministry to mankind. He has in mind to call upon people to believe, to repent, and to be baptized. There are increasing numbers who now follow him on that wise and with great sincerity of purpose.

Even so, the enemies of Enoch are increasingly bold and conspire against him, so that our further sojourn in the hill country may become troublesome.

With anticipation,
Mahijah

Greetings to My Friend with the Palsied Hand, Omner!

My servants, returning from your place again empty-handed, did report that you spoke with irritation about my words concerning the justice of Enoch, saying there was surely superior justice in your land. True, the land of Omner has a goodly measure of justice and mercy of which its inhabitants are rightfully proud. But whence cometh the notion of justice in the first place or the measuring rod to mete out to each man his measure? Justice in the land of Omner came from your father Omner's consulting with his own conscience. But even if you can sustain your father's system of justice, will your son do likewise? For evil erodes such mortal measuring rods.

Enoch preaches that only revealed standards give us true justice and true mercy. Mortal justice is worn away as the will of men is worn away or as each man persuades himself that his views are the thoughts of all men. The doing of any good surely carries its own reward, but perhaps as the followers of Enoch say, we cannot practice one principle of Jesus Christ, apart from all his other principles, and have full happiness. They say that all the principles of Jesus need each other, Omner, just as the people of Jesus need each other. Besides, justice is but one of a cluster of concerns to which Enoch addresses himself.

I paused for a period of several hours because, to my great delight, a letter from you was just delivered to me by your near-breathless bearers.

Omner, my beloved friend, our friendship is deep and sweet! It has been a fast friendship. Omner, if, as you say, men must walk in their own way as seems to them best, it will not disturb you if I choose a way different from your own. You will recall our jesting on one occasion about the saying that if one had no destination in life, it should not trouble him if he failed to get there? That I may now have a clearer destination in life will not offend you. Perhaps it can become a destination you will share.

I have a deep decision to make. The strange thing about this decision, Omner, is that while it is not at variance with logic and reason, it does not depend alone upon them either. Nor will the decision be made on a basis of mere feeling. It is a decision to be made by a form of knowing which lies somewhere beyond the realms of both thinking and feeling. I regret not being able to explain it. A man can know something and yet not be able to speak of that truth easily to another. Do you recall when you were sick and confined to your bed, sending me to the marketplace to lay hold upon a new servant of yours? You, knowing how he looked, could have found him quickly; but your description of him to me was not sufficient, and I failed to find him for you. Yet you knew how this servant looked! The tongue cannot tell some truths, Omner, even when we would will it otherwise.

If I do affiliate with Enoch and his followers, I am sure I will be a better friend of yours. Their love of their God seems to move these people to a greater love of their fellowmen, and Enoch is not only a preacher of righteousness, but also a performer of righteousness. The small band who follow him claim that among them liberty does not rob order, and order does not mock liberty. Surely such cannot be a harmful thing in a world that is otherwise growing so hard, Omner. You and I have both observed in times past the brutality we have seen all about us — to animals, which is so unnecessary, and to humans, which is so terrible. I see leers on the faces of the people in my city, but no smiles anymore. They seem to be without mercy, Omner.

No doubt we could resolve many matters if we could but see each other. I can only trust that your esteem for me is as mine for you, and that such esteem will endure both time and circumstance.

19

One thought as I close this communication: The claims of Enoch are so bold and so daring that, in one sense, I cannot lightly lay them aside. I will finally have to do just as Enoch says: I must choose! You can see throughout this epistle that for me, belief is near at hand. Already I have been among the most hesitant of Enoch's first hearers to make final determination concerning this man and his message. Being wealthy and of station, I fear I have reflected too much upon what I would give up and too little on what I might give to others. Discipleship with Enoch is not cheap nor without its costs.

To use human logic to explain to you why I am making these first tentative expressions of possible belief would be folly. There are stirrings and feelings inside me that are difficult to describe. I myself do not know what they mean yet or where they will lead. But I intend to follow them. That I cannot explain my feelings fully does not mean that they are inexplicable; we often know more than we can tell.

I can now understand why only the path of duty would persuade Enoch to leave his happy home.

It is also clear to me that Enoch did not call himself to preach to this people. He clearly feels called, and he preaches not as you once surmised, my friend, out of puffed pride or merely to make himself heard, but because of his deep sense of duty.

The followers of Enoch are becoming numerous. Yet if they choose to separate themselves from this city, it will not be out of fear, but that they might better pursue the ways of God. Should I join them, that need not be the end of our exchange of epistles, but I shall then be under the necessity of finding new ways to reach you.

I deeply desire that no gulf come between us, but I am also anxious to maintain my own integrity, as I wish you to maintain yours. Events are becoming a wedge between us; hence my double desire to send further word to you whenever and however I can. I will respond to your last message further only after I have pondered it more carefully.

Your concerned and faithful friend,
Mahijah

To My Esteemed Omner,
Joyful Greetings and Good Wishes!

This is the first communication written to you from inside the group of true believers who surround the Prophet Enoch. Yes, I call him a prophet now, for I fully feel and know that he is such. I have come to accept his Lord, Jesus Christ, the Savior Anointed, as my Lord!

When I first and belatedly expressed outwardly my belief in Jesus Christ, I quickly asked for help with my unbelief. It was as if I had unsteadily crossed a chasm of commitment and, once on the other side, found the view so breathtaking that at once, I shakily cried out for help.

Omner, I came to feel and to realize that I am a pilgrim on this planet and a stranger in all cities except in our little city upon a hill. Here I feel a deep belonging, and I now can feed on the rich revelations Enoch receives, for these not only teach us of higher ways, but also prepare us for a better world. Yet we do not hurry to heaven, for the straight and narrow path requires patience and persistence.

I have also come to accept what Enoch has preached as the plan of salvation, insofar as I understand it, whereby man may be saved through faith on Jesus Christ, through repenting of our sins, by being baptized for the remission of our sins, and by receiving the witness and guidance of the Holy Ghost.

I can imagine if not your surprise, at least your disappointment. These four simple, yet profound, things are but the beginning, not the end. As you could tell from my previous epistles, I was beginning to believe, but then it was a witness merely of my mind, which, though not unimportant, is not comparable to the witness of the Spirit delegated to attend the righteous that I have now received.

The work in which Enoch is engaged is, indeed, the work of the only true God. I applied the test that Enoch had given us, in which he promised that to all who would seek to choose, the Lord would give help both in making their decision and in standing fast in that decision, once made.

My own experiences brought me partway to this point; the violence, the corruption, the cruelty of the society of which you and I have been a part is in marked contrast to the goodness, the peace, the kindness and love that I experience as one of the true believers. Someday that time will come when every man who will not take his sword against his neighbor must needs flee unto this city for safety.

While in the world men delight in the weakness of another, in this small city the strong seek to strengthen the feeble knees of their neighbor and to lift up his weary arms. Of a truth, those who can bend their knees in prayer do not feel they are stooping when they bend to help a neighbor in need.

Of course, we feel the press of each other in a city of this size; one gets jostled in the crowd, but accepts such with good humor, rather than assuming malevolence on the part of another. At first we feel each other's elbows, but soon we learn to look into each other's eyes and into the radiant faces of those with whom we have made common cause.

As I ponder the teachings here, I am struck by these simple but powerful truths. In the teachings of men — without Christ at the center — there will soon be a slackening sense of service to others. Believing in a loving God who is perfect helps us to love our imperfect neighbors. I see now that the first commandment must be first and, therefore, the second commandment must be second, for without a knowledge of love of God and his help, our concerns for our neighbors would diminish. Men do not usually love a neighbor simply because he is there; some discover that he exists only after they become persuaded that God exists.

Whereas the world feeds on jealousy, here people are glad when others succeed and are never glad when others fail or fall into error. Omner, the generosity of neighbors in small things brings to pass big blessings and in so many ways. A person's small puffs of pride are best blown away by the breeze of brotherhood; left alone, these become enlarged and dark thunderclouds which drench all roundabout.

You should observe, Omner, how here they listen to each other instead of seeking to display their own learning. They are more willing to be impressed than they are eager to impress. Each seeks to do his share, that all may be equally yoked together in labor. Even the manner in which they help the needy enlarges the soul instead of the greed of him who is helped.

In place of covetousness, there develops generosity. Where there was indifference, there comes concern. Greed gives way to sharing, and the selfish lust for sensation is dissolved by pure charity.

This, for me, has been far more than the first blush of believing; it is a homecoming!

I desire to try to describe to you life within the small city, for we are now staying in one place (some say it will become a special city). I know not, save it is where I want to be. We have not withdrawn ourselves from the world in disdain; missionaries are being sent out to do just what Enoch began to do when he labored alone. I hope that I might have the privilege of preaching, but, selfishly, I am glad to be here for a season to gain strength, wisdom, and knowledge.

These are a special people whom I do not feel worthy to be among, and yet I feel a sense of belonging and purpose in life such as I have never felt before. We are helped on our way by having such forgiving friends, for when friends truly forgive us, it is so much easier to forgive ourselves. Some never stand before a more harsh and heartless judge than themselves.

Let me be honest with you, Omner. I hope one day you will join me. I shall not love you less if that is not your decision, yet I cannot but wish for you those blessings that are coming to me. I am hopeful that my letter will reach you and that you will reply soon.

Men may run to and fro in search of another way, Omner, but there is none. Kings and rulers come and kings and rulers go, but Christ is constant. Others may teach truths, but not those truths which matter most. Still others teach that which is pleasing to the carnal mind. All such teachings melt away as the mortal moments melt away and as the shadows flee at the break of each dawn. Of a truth, Omner, there is nothing out there but endless emptiness. Come, follow Christ to a land not only of milk and honey, but a land of liberty and love, a place of purpose and principles. Be no more a stranger!

Bad conditions can wear away even good men, Omner. When, in the judgment of God, the good can exist side by side with the wicked as do wheat and tares, God will permit it. But when, in his infinite wisdom, he chooses both to prepare and preserve a people, the righteous are withdrawn, and then things become much worse among the residue of people where you remain. Please consider my concern.

Your anxious friend,
Mahijah

My Esteemed and Inquiring Friend, Omner:

Though your previous and probing letter has already stirred me to reply, I soon realized that my last epistle omitted a matter of solemn significance, which I touch upon briefly now.

I would not have you ignorant, Omner, of one special condition that has aided greatly in the steady progress of this people. I refer to the loving regard the several generations, living side by side here, have for each other. This is no ordinary esteem that passes between these people, for they perceive themselves as carrying out divine purposes, which purposes both preceded their own birth and will persist after their passing. This creates feelings about the past, present, and future that take no note of time and that seem to seal these generations to each other with fastness never before known to me.

Moreover, not only is there the high esteem so evident in these relationships, but the living together of overlapping generations also calls into being a marked sense of community, and a moral momentum envelops all, yet with their consent. Who would have it otherwise, when the young in this city are taught not alone by parents, but by grandparents and great-grandparents alike? Many here have known Adam and other great patriarchs and can thus witness for themselves, as well as for those generations who follow them, about the constancy of God's purposes.

Had I not been so dull, I would have earlier perceived and written of this pervasive power of community that I fear even now I have feebly described; it accounts for so much of what is done so well among this people.

Your constant friend and concerned colleague,
Mahijah

Greetings to My Steadfast Omner!

Some seem to find no succor in the words of eternal life. There is in them no thirst for righteousness. I pray —

yes, pray — that you will be stirred by the Spirit to listen to the words of eternal life, though you disdain to reply. Here we are told that the righteous will enjoy the words of eternal life in this world and eternal life in the world to come, even immortal glory. Those who do not actually enjoy the words of eternal life are seldom moved to do the earthly deeds that make eternal life possible.

If in this mortal maze there was one who said simply there is a single solitary straight and narrow way out, and I will lead you, would you not go? Would you not listen? Nevertheless, some in that mortal maze cease trying to save themselves. Still others pretend that the pit is not a pit. Some curse God and wish to die, revelling strangely in their fate, as if they were a lost legion. Few there are who find that straight and narrow way. It is a way so simple, so direct, so easy that many will say it cannot be right, and refuse to follow. I truly desire that you not be blinded to the one way.

Even something as small as a man's thumb, when held very near the eye, can blind him to the very large sun. Yet the sun is still there. Blindness is brought upon the man by himself. When we draw other things too close, placing them first, we obscure our vision of heaven.

I do not mean to paint a picture of perfection for you, for we of this city are imperfect creatures. We feel very undeserving of God's blessings, yet we cannot but thank him for those bounteous blessings that are ours. Where we now feel affection and friendship for each other, Enoch teaches us that friendship will one day ripen into charity, the pure love of Christ, and that we will be of one heart.

When we were freshly received into the city from the world, many of our opinions and ways of living were still not shed. I believe there will come to us an even greater unity in the way we live as well as in the way we think, that we may be of one heart. I sense here an urgency, but no panic — a desire to move swiftly and surely to establish ourselves as a people, so that others may be drawn to this city of believers.

We enter the city hesitant and very imperfect, each of us bringing a burden of sin that can be lifted from us only by believing and being baptized with water and fire. Even then, our mortal appetites seem to persist, for perfection is a direction to be pursued in the process of time. Each of us must not only renounce evil, disengaging from doing wrong, but we must also engage anxiously in doing much good. Only then can a mighty change occur.

When a poorly clad beggar came into the city and, still in his old ways, saw an untended cloak, he took it. Then the owner of the cloak approached the beggar and gave him his coat also! The beggar first froze in fear, and then there was puzzlement in his eyes; then came tears of shame and gratitude; finally the two men wept together.

Some have come here and then departed, because their sorrow was not a godly sorrow that worked true repentance; theirs was the sorrowing of the damned, because they were not at home in either the realm of righteousness or in the society of sin.

Some have come to us and then have left our midst, for they have not been willing to be taught in temporal matters. Our commerce must be the commerce of Christ, for the morals of the marketplace matter and do find their way into families.

Enoch tells us that the wickedness in the world from which we have withdrawn may be the greatest wickedness among all of God's creations. How that saddens my heart, for with wickedness there is no happiness. Our missionaries report that many outside this city are without order and without civilization.

You will surely attest, Omner, that many of those with whom we had our dealings for so many years are men without affection. I could never decide whether many of our associates hated themselves and then hated mankind the more, or whether it was their contact with mankind, and their revulsion therefrom, that made them hate themselves.

Here it is greatly different. We meet together often to hear the word of the Lord from each other, particularly from our leaders. We deem it a privilege when Enoch himself is able to speak to us. We engage in praying and in fasting to prepare ourselves to listen.

But I would not have you think that our society is one in which there is no labor or work. We are kept busy with the chores of community life, but our minds are not allowed to wander away from our purposes. The simplicity of the doctrines and the rituals do not give us the excuse of complexity for failing.

Can you imagine the love and affection a man feels when there are so many anxious to administer to his needs? At first we selfishly accept this love in awe and wonderment. Then we are soon caught up in a desire to deal likewise with our fellowmen.

You rightly asked, Omner, if our emerging unity carries us farther forward than each man might go himself, and if so, if such progress is real. Each is blessed according to his keeping of the commandments; none is finally blessed solely because of the obedience of another. But, Omner, the subtle and wondrous efficiency of righteous unity is found in the manner in which it moves each man to do more than he ever imagined, or even wanted, to do himself. Seeing others pass a supposed breaking point without breaking, going a second mile with a burden they are only required to carry one mile, witnessing those falsely accused persist in sweet patience — there is a clear contagion in such things, Omner. One is simply inspired to do more, and his performance is sanctified for the welfare of his soul.

The helping graces involve all manner of quiet goodness. By noticing but ignoring the petulance of another, the gentle onlooker can indicate his awareness that the offender not only knows better, but will momentarily do better. The offender comes more quickly to his senses, whereas the way of the world causes a man to defend his wrong even though for one brief moment he is prepared to apologize. Thus the balm of brotherhood not alone keeps us from picking at the scabs of our errors, but lessens the making of such errors.

Another helping grace is simply speaking the truth in love. How that helps us all to listen! In like manner, when reproof is called for, the reprover shows forth afterwards an increase in his love of the reproved, that the latter be not swallowed up in overmuch sorrow.

The plan of salvation, Omner, tells us truly that we have wandered from a more exalted sphere; there is a better place and a better world to which we may, if we choose, return. Life in this city is but a foretaste of that future, and it stirs in me memories beyond memories. Omner, when there is peace, happiness, and love at home, men find it easier to join in those community enterprises that edify all. Indeed, when there is faith in a family and love at home, there is beauty all around. As I have previously written you at length, my own family joys have multiplied many times since we came to this special place. So it is beginning to be in the City of Enoch!

You may recall my description of Enoch in his first years as one who is not only humble, but shy. Now he is bold and yet without overbearance. I feel when his eyes fall upon me that they see through me as if I were transparent. Yet I do not sense in him a desire to judge me or to dominate me. I realize only now that the teasing question I first put to Enoch years ago about his origins truly sprang from my real desire to know, and not from sophistry.

He esteems his neighbors and his friends as himself and desires for each the joys of righteousness that he, Enoch, is experiencing.

Each of us finds a way for his talents to be so employed.

I have already been asked, for instance, to act as a scribe in preparing many of the communications to go out from Enoch to his people, that the word of the Lord may be written as well as spoken. It is a rare privilege because it keeps me close to the teachings of our living prophet. Most of all, it gives me some occasional association with Enoch himself. Yet it also keeps me from traveling in your direction, Omner.

Those among us who are builders of buildings, those who are gardeners, and those who tend vineyards, all are being assigned tasks to build our city, which we hope will one day be a city glorious, a city that the Lord will claim. There are no idlers here, Omner. The talented help the less talented, so that all may be edified together, temporally and spiritually. Here in this city the prophet and his leaders seek to educate our very desires, for God finally gives to each man the desires of his heart.

In this city we see the patient government of God. As the pilgrim comes to this city, the King is his host, and the Comforter, or the witness of the Father and Son, is his constant guide.

The Lord's work is work, but it is sweet labor. It is work usually done step by step in the process of time. Small daily duties well done have led to a big difference in just decades, for it is by small means that the Lord can bring about great things. There is no easy way to rush to righteousness. It is as if our very neighbor is all mankind, and thus we can see how much there is yet to do in the combining of our time and talents before we can truly be said to love our neighbors as ourselves.

Your lengthy but determined friend,
Mahijah

Dear Silent Omner:

Why am I confronted continually by this curtain of silence? My heart, which is so full in other ways, nevertheless aches in the realization that no word has come from you for the space of several years. My messengers tell of your stony stares as they deliver to you my epistles. Even so, I have continued to communicate with you and will continue to do so in hope that you will reply.

I have searched my memory in vain to see what offenses might have been given to you. Our friendship has outlasted much and it will outlast this silence, too, Omner. If I did not think an explanation of that sweet assurance would give you cause for fresh offense, I would tell even now how this comforting knowledge has come to me.

Ever your friend,
Mahijah

My Dear and Honored Omner, Greetings and Love!

I fear I did not do justice to your recent and broad inquiry about the manner of commerce here.

To deal justly in the marketplace, taking no advantage of another is no small challenge. Here it is done not by laws and regulations, which are usually multiplied without happy effect. Yet ours is a lively commerce — though it is the commerce of common concern where each is learning to esteem his neighbor as himself. Conscience sits as master of the market and each consults conscience. Where one is yet insensitive to justice in barter, he meets no spoken reproof, though he may see reproach in the kind eyes of those who look on. Often he who has taken advantage of another does not even complete his journey homeward from the market before, with heavy heart, he returns to put things aright.

Rules are useful, as you say, but these must merely mark where the borders of conscience end. Rules have a way of pushing conscience back, and yet farther back. Besides, Omner, each human and each human situation are sufficiently different that rules thus multiplied become

31

like the unpruned tree. A lively conscience can cut through to the justice of any situation.

I was pleased at your reference to how those of this city conduct themselves in their occasional trade in the land of Omner. We are not yet sufficient in all things here. The honesty shown by my brothers in your markets has caused respect, you say, and I am pleased. I am even more pleased that you report our men were true to the ways of the City of Enoch without imposing their ways on your kinsmen. We are taught here often of the evils of compulsion in any degree. We count on contagion, not compulsion, to win others to our ways.

I was heartened to hear in your last message how much you desired that the ways of our city become the ways of the land of Omner, such as the manner in which our children are reared. I wonder, even so, Omner, if you desire the obedience of youth without also desiring its true causes. The obedience in our children consists of respect, not fear, of their parents. Parents teach far more by example than by exhortation. Here, much time is spent in teaching children and youth to desire that which is right, so that our young may be safe when left to their own desires. They are truly taught to measure the consequences of what they want. One cannot have the harvest without planting that which must precede the plenteous harvest.

You groan, Omner, over the increasing evil in your land in which you say men are past feeling. Well you might fear for your fellowmen. You write that your countrymen are not steady and consistent. The adversary need not be consistent, Omner. Indeed, evil is not only erotic; it is erratic, since it must entice so many in such a multitude of ways. Thus, persuade a man possessed of one truth that he has all truth. Convince another that there is no truth whatsoever. Let another believe that all truths are of equal importance to man. Notice, Omner, that the result is the same in all cases: the searching for truth stops. Allow one person to think that no matter what he does, it is not wrong. Tell another that he has done wrong, but it is not serious. Persuade another that he has erred so gravely that there is no hope for him. Again, the result is the same: the sinning continues. The devil, Omner, is a liar and a cheat! Much work awaits, my beloved friend.

Till later,
Mahijah

Greetings to My Dear Friend Omner, Prince of His Land!

Your letter reached me after many months, and then I confess to being likewise tardy in response for even longer. Much has happened. I send this epistle to you in the midst of the many additional duties that have come upon me, but with no less love and no less interest in your welfare. Lest so much time pass again before I dispatch, I will write now in greater length, for even after the passing of so many years, I still have the harrowing memories with me of the awful chasm in our correspondence which once occurred.

Omner, ruler of your own land of Omner, this city is a theocracy, not an autocracy. I say this because my description of things here appears to have caused you to make wrong judgments. Enoch's profound power is not what it may seem to you. His leadership is the leadership of love and long-suffering; we are both free and safe here. His is also a righteous leadership. How wretched, by comparison, are the rulers you and I have witnessed who have gathered their guards about them and who have torn up the laws of worthy predecessors, causing great iniquity!

You put two questions to me in a past missive. You asked me how it is possible for me and others like me to believe in a Savior of mankind who is yet to come, to believe in someone who has not yet even been born after the

33

manner of men? It is true that the faith we are asked to develop is faith in events future, for Jesus Christ has not yet come to the earth to be crucified and to atone for the sins of mankind.

Enoch tells us that those who are to be born after Christ is born must develop a faith that involves believing back in time to the reality of Jesus' birth, his crucifixion, and the atonement. Whether one believes forward in time, as we, in this early dispensation, must do, or back in time, as our posterity in the dispensations to follow must do, is immaterial. In either instance, it is necessary that we believe in Jesus Christ, in his teachings, and in his unique mission.

Unless one wishes to surmise that distant disorder surrounds the order we all readily see in the stars and seasons, then man must ask whence such order came. They take the greatest chances who risk their souls by saying all things are done by chance. The divinity of Jesus Christ and his plan of salvation is not only the best explanation of things—it is the *only* explanation of all things! Here we do all things in his name. Enoch even prays to God, the Father, in the name of Jesus Christ, as he has been instructed to do.

Besides, beloved Omner, time is measured only to man, not to God. The prophets of God who live now speak of a time yet to come and give their witness concerning events to happen then. One day prophets, I am told, will give their witness as to events that have already happened. When one sees and then witnesses by the Spirit, as Enoch does, his vision is endless and it is as if there were no time. No forward, nor backward.

You must begin, friend of so many years, at the beginning with at least a desire to believe, and then let this desire work in you. You can test the doctrines of Jesus by your own experience, so that you can witness for yourself that they are true. This I have done. Our mere desire to believe can then become belief. Our belief moves on to faith. Next, as we have personal experiences with the truths of the gospel of Jesus Christ, our faith becomes knowledge in those things, and our witness is personal and powerful.

What I write of is no mystical experience—it is very real, for each day I see all about me the fruits of commandment keeping.

Having seen what I have seen, if I did not desire that the whole world be persuaded of the rightness of the religion of Enoch, I would be no friend to mankind.

Those here who are wiser than I (and such are legion) tell me that this city may exist for a time to draw men unto Jesus Christ, but that the more part of mankind will nevertheless be unpersuaded. This gives me a heavy heart, especially when I have friends, like you, Omner, whom I would gladly see drawn to Jesus Christ.

Not only do we gain greater happiness ourselves when we are righteous, but we also help our neighbor in subtle ways. How often the weaknesses in one man become a temptation to another man! My desire for wealth and gems can cause another man's envy; my temper has, at times past, dissolved your patience. One man's incontinence destroys what little is left of a righteous woman's resolve. One person's lust becomes another's way to wealth. A man's drunkenness becomes another man's excuse for Sabbath breaking to enlarge his vineyards. So it goes, Omner. So much can be done in concord that is hard to do alone. Besides, the virtues Enoch exhorts us to develop require us to ever be with one another. How can hermits practice brotherhood?

You made a point in your communication of so many months ago: you asked why I could believe in anything so simple. You even chided me with the reminder that I was once a student of the philosophies and the affairs of men. In this you are correct. But by looking back, I see that I was always looking beyond the mark, missing the obvious things that are so plain and so precious. God, in his love for each of us, is determined to save all whom he can; he does not want the way back to his presence to be complicated.

Intellectual embroidery is but an unreliable frill; the hardy and homely cloth of truth is to be found in the gospel of Jesus Christ. The very simpleness and easiness of the way do seem to deter some from entering the gate. Perhaps that is your situation. The philosophies of the world at their best are but strands of truth, several times diminished. Some men are delighted to take such threads, weaving these inferior strands into tapestries in which they glory more than in the whole truth itself.

The harsh reality, Omner, is that mankind must choose between opposites, between light and darkness, between truth and falsehood, between righteousness and unrighteousness, between happiness and misery. All of these choices are really simple. How delighted the adversary is when he can divert men from deciding about these first things and keep them busy with second, third, and fourth things. As I fear, my good friend Omner, he has so done with you!

It is not necessary for you to understand the mysteries inside the simple realities of life. The sunshine that causes your crops and trees to grow is not something you can explain, Omner. Yet you depend on sunshine. The regular coming of the rain that gives you water and that makes your crops grow is a blessing you cannot explain. Yet you accept it. You do not refuse food simply because you cannot explain the seasons or make yourself the seeds you have planted.

Repentance takes care of the past, faith the future, and the Holy Ghost helps us with today. The Holy Ghost can be our constant companion. It enlarges our conscience. It helps us to see the truth of all things, including the truth

36

in the transactions of the marketplace. It sharpens our eyes to see the needs of others who would otherwise be obscure. It quickens our pulse of pure passion, stirs us to action to assist others whom we might otherwise pass by and notice not. With this great gift, whether one consults his heart or his mind, the precious and practical counsel that comes forth is the same: we can receive such directions daily, even hourly.

Yet, I feel for you, inasmuch as I formerly pondered many times on the seeming simpleness and easiness of the way. Belief and faith do not require a man to cease using his reason. Use the power of your mind, Omner, but let your heart be opened to the influence of the Spirit through mighty prayer. Take the first faltering steps of faith. Choose before it is too late, my dear Omner!

One's acknowledgment of the need for divine help frees him from being hedged about by his own constraints. A man so humbled will not only listen the more to God, but may start listening also to his manservant—and doing the latter may be enough in some circumstances to set things aright.

Your friend in conviction and exhortation,
Mahijah

To Omner, My Beloved Friend, Greetings!

I would share with you some observations that may appeal to your mind, even though it is your heart that must finally be touched. Yet we must be sufficiently taught before the Spirit can testify to us of the truth of that which has been taught.

I am astonished at the efficiencies of righteousness. By this I mean, Prince Omner, that the great governmental systems built up in the cities you and I have known are perpetually preoccupied with the pain of obtaining compliance from citizens toward their government and toward each other. Servants are piled upon servants and functionaries check on other functionaries. Much wealth is spent to strive to insure that men deal justly one with another.

The city of the Lord is different wherein we seek not only that which is better, but that which is best. Filled as our city is with people who are increasingly of one heart and of one mind and who are moved by the same basic beliefs, there is need for less and less in the way of structure to see that people do their duty toward each other. Here we do not divert people from their own labors into wasteful secondary tasks; basic love and honesty obtain increasingly between our people.

When the inner man is changed, we have less and less need for outer controls. Men here do not hold back from doing their duty one toward another, from being honest one to another, because they love each other! They love each other even more deeply because they keep the first great commandment, to love the Lord their God with all their heart, mind, and soul. When men do not have a mind to injure one another, there is no need for sentries over society; here men pay their debts, often paying back even more than they borrow.

Here fathers know that their chief duties are to God, to family, and to this city. They prize their wives and children as eternal possessions to be cultivated more tenderly and diligently than any earthly crop. Children not only hear their father's faith spoken, but also see it in the actions of daily life; and beholding the faith of their fathers, they are exceedingly glad. Here the natural joy of children, who are whole from the foundation of the world, is fully joined to acquired joy of parents.

If we did not live the simple, yet challenging, commandments of God, we should not be a happy people. There are no contentions, disputations, envyings, strifes, and tumults. Nor are there whoredoms, lyings, or lasciviousness here. There are no robbers, murderers, or factions. We are one. We are the Lord's!

A man who is too busy to notice a neighbor also has no time to smell the flowers. Smallness of soul keeps us from contemplating both bird and brother, when God would have us exult over all his creations.

Even as I write, Omner, I sense that while I am describing life here, mine are words that come from within something holy. Yet you, reading my words, are, nevertheless, outside that which I seek to describe. Thus, my words may merely fall to the ground, when I desire to speak with the voice of a trumpet.

Ponder but one matter, Omner: how the women and children here rejoice because fathers and husbands are chaste. You and I have seen many times elsewhere the heartbreak of whoredoms, wherein the tender hearts of children and wives are pierced with deep wounds. Such wives become walking tombs of torment. Indeed, if the City of Enoch were a city of chastity only, how great would that blessing be even so! But the Lord's city is even more than a chaste city, for our chastity but manifests our other beliefs as well, such as our belief in a life to come. I am fully persuaded, Omner, that when a people have a slackening of belief in man's immortality, immorality will then increase among them. Without respect for God, they will have little respect for themselves.

In this city we learn from each other, being taught much by our friends. One such happy circumstance was a man new to our city who came to us much worried by his lust of mind. He was desirous of doing that which is right, yet his past determinations to purify his imaginings had ebbed like the tide. It was after yet another such moment that I partnered with him in prayer. As he sought the Lord mightily and steadily, I knelt at length by his side. I both felt and saw him gather strength such as never had been his before, that he might make an end to his lapses into lust.

Forgetting not his fervent petitions, he thereafter did these things: when evil entered his mind and heart, he made no place for it to tarry, but at once turned his thoughts to things of virtue, that light might dispel darkness. He likewise at once sought how he might serve others, that his energies would be turned away from what he might do to please himself and toward the fresh considerations that flow from seeking the welfare of others; and thus he dallied not with temptation, managing ere long to look upon women not as a pleasure to be contemplated, but as his sisters.

I was a nearby witness to the manner in which this friend did make strong determination to be chaste of mind and heart, persisting in that promise and anguishing his soul no more with determination laid upon determination. Thus the energy of his soul could be expended in good causes, being no more wearied down by endless enticements.

Omner, I do not say that to do such is easy, but it is necessary. Such can be done in like manner in whatsoever things sorely trouble a man's soul. Of a truth, temptation is not a gate that can be opened by force of arms; it opens only inward, as moved by the arm within, for each man is the gatekeeper of his soul.

Everyone here, in seeking the interest of his neighbor, seeks the larger interest. As a man blesses his neighbor, he also blesses himself, but the contrary is not always so. Let a person or a people persistently seek only their own interests, and there will finally come both a poverty of purse and a shrinking of soul.

I would not have you believe that all is easy herein, or perfect. It would be wrong to think that life in the City of Enoch is an idyllic, undisturbed, tranquil scene with nothing to do but to sit about and talk of truth. There are duties to be done, skills to put in service. Because neighbors love neighbors, each man learns his duties. For each, his work is his love made manifest for mankind.

We soon learn here that it is not enough to abstain from acts adverse to our fellowmen; we must also be anxiously engaged in good causes that lie unattended and all about us every day. At first perhaps one is almost too conscious of trying to help others and, therefore, his Christianity is too conspicuous and even condescending. It is a great joy to learn later how to help gladly and quietly and without acclaim. By being busy in the daily duties of life here, one almost loses consciousness of his progress. Otherwise, we would be forever pulling up the flowers to see how the roots are doing.

In this city the citizens are more concerned with the truthfulness of their utterances than with their manner of speaking. They give more thought to the content of their speech than they do to smoothness in their speaking. This delightful difference accounts for much of the happiness here.

To name but one such example, in touching upon the forgetting of wrongs done us, I have learned by sad experience that there is no expiation in retaliation; vengeance not only prolongs conflict, but also deepens and widens it. Thus, forgetfulness and forgiveness, by being intertwined, make strong the chords of brotherhood.

Eternal things are always done in the process of time. Men are ripened in righteousness as the grain is ripened. Each process requires rich soil and the sunlight of heaven. Time is measured only to impatient men. Direction is initially more important than speed. Who would really want momentum anyway, if he were on a wrong course?

If men make prior place for things other than Christ, they have failed to make the one choice that will free them from the trap of time.

Learning here in this special city is a mixture of duties and doctrines, for if we believe the things Enoch has taught

41

us, we must also do them. Here what begins as a duty soon becomes a delight. In happiness there is more energy to expend. With misery, there is first a holding back in hesitancy and then a falling back in despair.

Do not be vexed by our city apart, Omner. The issue is not our separation from our fellowmen, for in the wisdom of the Almighty, such separation is sometimes necessary for a season to prepare or to preserve a people. Those who bemoan or belittle our separation should first ponder their own separation from God. Without first seeking and acknowledging his Fatherhood, there can be no everlasting brotherhood of man.

You wrote sometime past of the ostracism that is coming to you. It can be a blessing when men separate you from their company, Omner, for their reproaching of you is not friendship lost, but opportunity gained to see them in their true character.

I testify now, Omner, of the living prophet Enoch. He is not only more pure than the clever men of the world, but he is much more interesting. Righteousness increases the uniqueness of our presence, but sin sinks us into sameness. Where there is beauty of person and personality, there is the capacity to appreciate beauty in others (and in the world), but also a determination to add to the beauty of one's environment. This is so with Enoch. I must confess, however, that each time I have the privilege of being in his presence, I *do* think of him as being perfect; for if he has faults, they are not discernible to me. Yet he himself seems unaware of his righteousness, for he is so humble and is so anxiously engaged in the building of this city or, more accurately, this people.

But Enoch had to be in command of himself before he could command the elements. God gives his power only to those by whom it will be safely and sweetly used. Once our will accords with his, there is no longer any reason for God to withhold his power from men.

You must not suppose that ease has been the lot of Enoch. Many a snare has been laid for him, and many a trial has been met and conquered. How else could he say to us that often we receive no witness from God until after the trial of our faith? Thus, Enoch's great faith has kept him pure — not the neglect of the adversary.

Enoch knows and has taught us that the powers of heaven cannot be handled except upon the principles of righteousness. They cannot be used to gratify our pride or ambition or to control the children of men. Enoch, therefore, leads by persuasion and by long-suffering (lo, how many years now has he loved and led his people?). His love for his fellowmen is unfeigned, and virtue garnishes his thoughts without end. Thus he can walk and talk with confidence when he is in the very presence of the Lord. Enoch not only gives wise counsel, but inspires ever better conduct in others.

Even now Enoch is preaching a new and hard doctrine among us. He speaks of one remaining sacrifice that each of us must be willing to make. I know not fully what he means.

I must make an end to writing and be about my duties. Be assured of my love and of the sincerity of the convictions that long since brought me into this band of believers. Accept of my humble witness that Enoch is a prophet.

Zion, Omner, is where the pure in heart dwell and where there is joy of countenance. By contrast, in hell there are no smiles!

You will recall that many years ago in a previous epistle I had hoped that you might come quickly to me because I sensed that I might be beginning to believe. I was deeply disappointed you did not wait upon me at that time, but now I am glad that nothing interfered then with the great and significant step I took in my life. Yet I must warn my neighbors in mildness and meekness and not with overbearance, and if I ever had a neighbor whom I loved and love still, it is you, Omner!

Your distant but ever affectionate friend,
Mahijah

To Dear Omner, My Once and Always Friend, Salutations!

I wrote you long months ago of Enoch's telling us that there was yet another commandment we must live that many of us might find hard to bear. We now know what that commandment is: we must give over all our goods and possessions, sharing them fully with each other, so that all may be equal in goods and substance. We who have laboriously learned not to withhold affection and esteem from each other must now no longer hold back our goods. Enoch promises that if we will do this, there will be no poor among us, for so many of those newly come to this city are poor, and yet they have heard Enoch's words gladly. Enoch has come among us more than ever before to exhort us regarding this new commandment.

Yes, Omner, you, who watched me husband and enlarge my fortune so carefully for so long, would be puzzled. Yet those of us who now have begun to be of one heart and of one mind must begin to be one in the things of this world.

Enoch tells us that it is not given that one man should possess that which is above another, wherefore the world lieth in sin. I have never before thought of these differences among men as a source of sin. Yet surely, those who have had their minds diverted to the care and attention of their possessions are often inclined to pride themselves on being above their neighbor. If our possessions are greater than those of our neighbors, we think that we ourselves are greater than our neighbors.

Moreover, those who have little are often inclined to

44

canker their souls with greed and envy. Thus, our hearts are either where our treasure is, or worse, where someone else's treasure is. So much of mankind's talents and thoughts are enthralled with things instead of truths. Tithing, about which I wrote you previously, has helped prepare us for this higher way, and so have the morals of our marketplace where men do not seek to enlarge their profit from the necessities of others.

Even this hard commandment is given to us so that we might live it voluntarily and not out of force or constraint. Some who could practice cooperation but not consecration here have freely left our midst. This is one of the great joys of life in the City of Enoch. Freedom and free agency are valued herein. Things are not imposed upon us. We do things out of devotion, not docility. We accept new teachings as steps to be taken if we are to draw ever closer to our God, and, therefore, we undertake to do our duties gladly, learning even as we obey.

When some who had been so righteous in other ways were counseled to give all they had to the poor, they went away sorrowing because their possessions were so great. Yet, if we truly ponder our circumstance, it must become clear that God gives us, first, breath, and second, the perishable gift of time. He then gives us increase. Now he asks only that we return his temporal gifts as evidence of our capacity to consecrate to him all things whatsoever we possess. But even as we yield, so much more is given to us in other blessings. God is a generous landlord, Omner! We are but his stewards.

We now see clearly, as pertaining to our goods and possessions, that unless we are equal in earthly things, we cannot be equal in heavenly things. We can have goods in common because we first have Christ in common. Only an uncommon people can have their possessions in common, and even then the challenge is very real and constant.

When men desire to be distinguished by rank, what

they really seek is not only recognition but to be distinguished from others, whether by wealth or wisdom. By separating themselves from the multitude, they presume a preeminence. But the work of the Lord is to be done among multitudes as he himself will do during his earthly ministry.

Yet it is not easy, for each of us has possessions we value highly, but which we must lay aside if we are to be true disciples. We may be impatient or even amused at the challenge this new commandment poses for others. Why should a man who cultivates vineyards find the giving up of his lowly pruning shears so hard? Why does he not yield these shears quickly? Yet each finds his own circumstances different and trying. I have seen, for instance, some for whom the giving up of costly apparel is a great trial. I have never cared that much for raiment, as you know. But before I let myself be much amused at such travail in others, I must note that it was not easy for me to surrender my precious gems, which, as you know, I have husbanded over many years. I have enjoyed the mere handling of them and the passing of them through my fingers. The sense of possession has given me a sense of security, and I miss my gems, now that they are gone. I once spoke almost reverently of them as works of nature to be prized, as I watched sunlight dance through their prisms. It was a near lust for me!

Fortunately, I have been so caught up in my duties and in the joy we have daily in association with each other that service to others has helped me to surrender my gems more easily. But finally, Omner, there has come the convincing and sober realization that they were not mine after all! It is easier to give up that which is not ours.

Of course, Omner, all do not seek to accumulate possessions because of greed alone. For some, displaying prowess in trading is an adventure not unlike an adventure at arms. But such are, unknowingly, turning aside from the great adventure of affording affection in their own family or are missing the likewise stern challenge of expressing esteem for their neighbors.

More than once have I witnessed those here who were once of rank in the world give way gladly to make place at a feast for those whom they might once have scoffed at because of their lowliness of station. Those who have in the past pushed others in order that they might further their own ambitions are now not only civil, but willingly deferential. This can be so because among the things we also have in common is the sweet knowledge that we are all children of God, our Father. Given that glad reality, there is no need to prove anything to anybody after the manner of the world.

The sense of eternity that likewise pervades this place lessens those of our anxieties which are rooted in the thing we men call "time." Here busyness, in order to be seen of men, calls forth only knowing smiles, not plaudits.

You will remember my mentioning how the artisans and craftsmen among us have been given their tasks. Beautiful new buildings are now arising, the architecture and splendor of which please beyond compare the mortal eye. We hope we are pleasing to the Lord. The gardens in our villas are of incomparable beauty. In the midst of all this achievement, no man esteems himself above his neighbor, for each has gifts.

The artisan is not looked down upon by those who have duties to oversee him. If ever the puzzled and perplexed critics of the City of Enoch could be objective and not merely angry at that which is good, they would see that believing in Jesus Christ brings out the individual talents of men in a way that is not otherwise possible. Thus in the emerging excellence of the ways and wonders in Enoch's city, I perceive that those who worship the Creator are exceedingly creative. It is so much easier, however, to learn both *what* to do and *how* to do it, when we first know

47

why things must be done at all. Too often, Omner, the talented withhold their talents because of pique or confusion as to *why* they must help others. Here that confusion is dispelled with dispatch.

The dullness in the world is the dullness of degraded people believing in degraded doctrines. The world you and I knew together is not, of course, without its achievements or its points of beauty, but these are the work of a few. Their monuments to beauty mark occasional individual talent, not a way of life. Such isolated beauty is too often later dimmed by time, but at once by unharmonious surroundings.

Not so here in the City of Enoch, the splendor of which grows each day. Ours is not the splendor of the rich who create by the misery of the poor. This splendor springs from the work of all our people, each of whom revels in the talents and accomplishments of the other. Each is inclined to glorify God rather than himself, and to thank God first for giving talents that make such beauty possible.

We once saw this city only through eyes of faith; we now see it emerging with our natural eyes. And we are glad!

Please send me word, Omner, of your own struggle for faith. I pray daily for you and would come to you if duties permitted. I renew my plea to send missionaries to you. In your skepticism, you have said often that seeing is believing. Believing is also seeing, Omner!

Yours in the love and peace of the Lord,
Mahijah

To Omner, Still the Friend of My Heart:

You asked about the love that is here and whether it is real. Perhaps my descriptions of life here have been too casual. I would not have you believe that this great principle has been easy to live.

It is usually easier for us to love those whom we should love most naturally—our parents, our children, our husband or wife. Yet in the world even that natural love is often twisted. Here in our city we have also been asked to love even when such love is not returned. Here we have needed to learn to love strangers, since we all came as strangers. Here we have been taught to love even those who were once, or would otherwise be, our enemies.

It has been helpful for me, as I have struggled to enlarge my soul in love, to love God first—as much as I can—for he is perfect and because he loves us, and we therefore start by seeking to be like him. It is also helpful in the process of learning to love others more deeply to realize who others really are—our eternal brothers and sisters, our friends of the future, our peers of a past beyond the pale of mortal memory.

The fruits of love are often quickly ripened and so satisfying to the taste that love draws us in search of more. It is also helpful when others simultaneously try to love us. Several times in my smallness of soul I have resented a particular person, but that person has rescued me from my frailties, because he has nevertheless demonstrated afresh his love for me. My shame has soon changed in a resolve to do better. Further, there are about us exemplars who have moved a greater distance down the pathway of love. It has been helpful to see them, to experience them, and to feel their love.

I soon found that if I could but be patient even if others were impatient with me, if I could but absorb unkind words without responding at once in resentment, the genuine regrets of the other person would move them to kindness. If I had responded otherwise, they would soon have been both angry at me and disappointed with themselves.

Omner, in your wit you said that in the City of Enoch we seem to have all the answers. We also have proper questions. I have learned, for instance, through sad experience to check my conduct by asking myself in the midst of the stress of daily duties such simple questions as: "Whose needs am I really trying to meet?" Sincerely asking such a question often brings forth a much-needed reminder.

As I involve myself in the give and take of life here, I first check for the presence of pride in the midst of my emotions. Often when I feel wounded, upon sober reflection, I see that it is my pride, not a principle, that is the cause.

Therefore, Omner, to strive to love my Father in Heaven—with all my heart, mind, and strength—and my neighbor as myself puts Mahijah in proper perspective. Thus, on the first two great commandments that have been given to us by the Lord hang all the other laws and commandments.

Further, when I speak to you, Omner, of the unity here, and how we are of one mind and one heart, this must cause puzzlement in your soul, as it would in mine if I were trying to understand this city while standing outside its walls. Indeed, it is only by being inside that we can experience such unity, and even then it is difficult to explain.

The unity and oneness we have is facilitated by our having the gift of the Holy Ghost, for he encourages us in doing righteous things and also constrains us from manifesting our pride. This help is given in seemingly minor matters and also in truly weighty matters. Our experience here also teaches us to be patient with one another. Likewise, things that may seem unclear become clear; things that at first seem obscure become obvious.

Our unity is not the unity born of compulsion or of mindless rapport, but of the realization that such unity is a necessity.

Omner, you would not criticize a group of people who sought the same high ground in the midst of a flood; you would not see their presence in one place as an unintelligent act, for they came together in order to be saved. So it is here.

Life here is life in a large, affectionate, and unified family. Love in a family does not diminish the freedom of each member thereof; our unity does not jeopardize our individuality. Undivided, we are multiplied. Being of one heart and one mind permits no divorce between knowing and feeling in the City of Enoch.

Dissent is not present here. There is no need for dissent over doctrine, for the doctrines are perfect, and those who subscribe to these doctrines have freely elected Enoch's city as their abode. To dissent because of injustice in the presence of justice would be foolishness. To dissent because of pride is unnecessary, since all are humble. To dissent merely to display one's freedom would be a mark of one's bondage to pride. To dissent merely for the sake of dissent is not a mark of maturity. In other words, here, Omner, dissent would serve no purpose. Children, once they learn to walk, do not resume crawling again merely to prove that they can crawl!

It helps greatly to do first things first, not only because these are most important, but because the order of things does matter. The process of believing together is the beginning of the unity of our minds. The process of repenting brings us to a greater unity in the manner of our living. The process of being baptized shows our willingness to submit to a common ordinance, that we might become an uncommon people. Receiving the gift of the Holy Ghost brings us to a unity in perceiving things as they really are and in the performing of our daily duties.

Prayer keeps us ever mindful of our dependence on God. It is so easy to forget our present blessings as we pursue new blessings. In our meetings we recount our own blessings, and as we hear the blessings of others, we

51

both feel and see the accumulations of affection from God to his people.

The people of the world, in contrast, try to choose noble consequences without also choosing the noble ways of life that lead to those consequences. We cannot choose peace and then labor for peace apart from other conditions. Armies may slay each other with the sword by day, but by night slumber, but an adulteress will be cut continuously by the sword of her conscience and have no peace. Peace is based not alone on justice, but also on the process of self-discipline and selflessness without which peace is impossible. Contrariwise, where people's thoughts are selfish, they will, one way or another, find cause to feel deprived or injured.

Omner, many times in the years spent in this city I have been moved to tears, sometimes from sadness over a sin of mine, but more often because of the indescribable joy that washes over me again and again. Miracles have moved me to tears, but when I weep most fervently, it is because of the goodness of God when the mighty change of heart occurs in one of his children. Perhaps mentioning one such circumstance will suffice.

There has been a man of particular mark and sway among us who was nearly consumed in his desire for praise. He partook deeply of the praise of the world while yet out in the world. His ways thus vexed his companions here almost daily, though they bore up admirably. Having not seen him for several seasons, I at last saw him in a setting where an achievement of worth pertaining to our harvest was being celebrated. A good measure of what had been done was done by him (for he is possessed of many talents), but no notice was being taken of his contribution nor even of his presence. None was sought by him, either. Then I saw him rejoice quietly over the achievement that blessed so many. Tears ran down his face, unnoticed except by me. Yet he gloried not in himself, but in what had been

52

done. Then I wept. When I pondered upon what had brought him to this new point and how he must have struggled to make quiet determination to do differently, I marveled at the ways of God. Then when I saw him slip away quietly from the group, having received no praise whatsoever, yet having true joy in his heart, I wept again.

My words are but the musings of a mere man, but they enlarge upon the descriptions I send to you, descriptions that otherwise must seem to you to glow so brightly that you may question my credibility and integrity. If you do still question, even now, it gives me yet another reason to suggest, as I have so many times, that you come, see, and experience for yourself. Experiment upon my words!

As the owner of many large vineyards, Omner, you know that you must expect the fruit of the selfsame plant you plant. For what man plants vines and is then surprised or angry when wheat does not appear? In order for men to partake of the fruit of felicity, they must plant the seeds thereof.

Therefore, Omner, do not suppose that a single skill, one attribute, or one tremendous talent could make such a city. Many seemingly small things are combined here which together make a big difference. Things are fitly framed together.

Thank you, Omner, for your generosity in suggesting that in recent years this friend writes with more conviction and competence. You also kindly suggested that I seem more humble. If so, I have so much to be humble about!

Your friend in witnessing assurance,
Mahijah

To My Dear Omner, with Concern but Undiminished Love, Greetings!

My heart is heavy with the word that you have rejected the missionaries of Enoch sent to declare the truth to you.

I am told you said to them that life is shatteringly senseless and that, therefore, there could be no plan of salvation. Omner, you are too drowned in the disorder of your land to recognize divine design. I testify to you that life is no labyrinth; mortality is no maze if a man possesses the gift of the Holy Ghost to guide him. Your sense of onrushing darkness can be dispelled only by the light of the gospel. Do humble yourself, that all will not be lost for you! Could it be that the excuse you gave was not your real reason?

Enoch's emissaries, in love of you, said that they feared you expected the Prophet would bid you do some great thing—something dramatic—instead of merely believing and being baptized. Why, my friend, do you prefer the grandiose and vague to the simple and specific? Ordinances are necessary milestones in this mortal march, marking and showing the way, signifying those things which are both endings and beginnings, such as baptism, which signifies both a burial and a resurrection.

As for the gift of the Holy Ghost, a supposed truth-seeker, like you, more than all others, should crave the Comforter who will help you to know the truth of all things. Do you really want to know, Omner?

Obedience to ordinances testifies of our trust in God, just as Enoch did as he was once bidden of the Lord, humbly anointing his eyes with clay and washing them so that he might see a special vision. The Lord loves both the teachable and the unteachable, but is it through the obedience of the teachable that God can help these helpers, that all might be benefitted thereby.

Please do not think me condescending, for I care for you. In the language of Adam, Man of Holiness is the name of Jesus Christ, and surely none is fully holy but Christ. Surely not I, for I am vexed by my sins, but steadily seek their cessation.

The meetings I have mentioned to you wherein we instruct each other and bear testimony have always been a joy. But now as the city rises above us, they are meetings that move me to tears of gratitude. I am often not able to contain myself. In many ways, my greatest anxiety occurs in my own role as a scribe when I try to portray our city, for my words are pitifully inadequate, and I am embarrassed even to set them forth. Yet that is my task.

It gives me great joy to know that my gems made possible the purchase of materials out of which one of our loveliest buildings is now being built, with fountains and shrubbery to gladden the heart and to please the eye.

I now see that the act of divesting himself of those material things which otherwise set him apart from others is the final measure of a man. Those who have adequate for their own needs soon find that anything beyond that point is encumbering wealth — wealth that should be put to effective use in the care of those who have less. I see now, too, why this people had to be separated, for the laws of men would have been used to vex and to try us sorely had we tried to have all things in common while yet remaining in the world.

In the City of Enoch there are now no poor, because each man esteems his neighbor as himself, having the same constant concerns for his neighbor as he has for himself. Prospered as we were, the ninety-nine were not able to rest until the one had the food, the clothing, and the shelter he needed.

There is greater efficiency when people band together in love and truth. They produce more in cooperation, and there is thus more to share. The believer in the gospel of work is also more productive. Finally, there are no indolent rulers to take away the fruits of men's labor.

There are no poor among us because all have a greater desire to give than to take, a stronger desire to share than to receive. If we are too much attached to the goods of this world we err, because they cannot be taken with us to that next place.

55

I am deeply saddened by the reports of our missionaries and others who are newly come to the ranks of the city about the growing wickedness and violence out in the world, and the bloodshed there. I am concerned for your safety, though I know you are well established and have your guards about you and your possessions. I pray for you even so, Omner.

The residue of the people are becoming absorbed in themselves, full aliens from God, as they are consumed in sin and wars; their only thoughts are for themselves, for today, for pleasure, and for revenge. The time seems at hand (of which I wrote to you decades ago) when all who will not take up his sword against his neighbor must flee unto Zion for safety. Come to this Zion, Omner!

Perhaps the worst curse that finally falls upon those who are hard of heart and who fight against God is the curse of being consigned to be with each other. Hardness of heart comes first in the form of forgetfulness, for memory is the mother of feeling. When a people can no longer be stirred up to remembrance, they become past feeling. Their hearts become like shells and, finally, stones.

Evil always seeks company, for it cannot be by itself alone. Satan detests solitude, for solitude turns him in upon himself, reminding him of what glories might have been. Thus, when Satan laughs as if to mock mankind, he only mocks himself. His laughter is hollow laughter that proceeds from the emptiness of evil which envelops him.

I renew my plea for you to listen to our teachings. I rejoice still in the reports received sometime ago that in meetings where counsel was taken about how the people of the world might come up against the City of Enoch, your voice was raised, saying we should be let alone. I thank you for that. Though the Lord protects us, it was good of you so to speak. Your having spoken forth was one of the reasons I am concerned over you, because the ways of the adversary are such, as men's hearts grow increasingly hard, that any who seem to have any tolerance whatsoever for the people of God will be viewed with anger by those who would destroy us.

Have no fear for us, Omner; the Lord watches over us. You have heard reports of how when Enoch has spoken the very earth has trembled? From the beginning, years ago, those who would have laid hold on him have always fallen back in fear, unable to pierce him, even though Enoch's words pierced them deeply.

Enoch does not glory in himself for his marvelous achievements. He is quick to give praise to God and to others. He seems everywhere present in our city. None are of so little consequence as to go unnoticed by him, even though we now number in the thousands. Now I must make an end to writing this missive. Please thank your messenger, for once outside our walls he risks his personal safety to bring this to you. I have thanked him, but if you would also, it would gladden my heart the more.

I know in the beginning you chided me for the physical separation of Enoch's people from the world about us. It has been necessary, Omner, as you must now see; for now we are able to withstand the wickedness of the world. I am told that even the people of large stature, called giants, have stood far off in great perplexity about this city. They would surely have fallen upon us if they were not so fearful of the glory of the Lord that hovers over us.

There is no fear in the City of Enoch. Men fear, Omner, only when there is not sufficient love in their hearts. Perfect love casts out fear, and he that fears is not made perfect in love. There is liberty in love. Only when men are not fearful can they be anxiously and fully engaged in bringing to pass much righteousness, turning outward instead of inward.

In your city, Omner, the divisions among men but mirror the divisions within each man. Only when the war within each man has first ended can there be real peace.

I make an end of writing to you, but never of praying for you!

Your friend in prayer and humble pleadings,
Mahijah

My Dear Omner:

Of the many responses over the long years of our correspondence since we have been so much apart, no words have touched me so much as your words which came just now, telling of the loss of your heir and eldest son. Truly yours is the heart of a tender father. I marvel that your own tenderness survives still in the growing hardness of your land.

In your expression of sorrow—in which I truly join—there was more than a desire to believe. Please forgive, therefore, my rejoicing even as you mourn. My hope is that in the midst of your lamentations, there might emerge another sound—the sound of a still, small voice to which you will listen with your mind and your heart together.

Omner, you who have dealt justly with so many others, now must deal justly with yourself. Do not shut out the words of your Eternal Father who would speak to you, his son. There may be no better chance for that glorious reunion than now, inasmuch as you, too, are an anguished father who would one day be reunited with his mortal son!

In love and shared sorrow,
Mahijah

To Omner, Wherever You May Be in the Wide and Troubled World, Felicitations!

I write to you the sooner because of the tremendous events of the last few days. I am hopeful my last letter reached you before these occurred. We hear that the people in the world are astonished about the great land that has so suddenly risen up out of the very sea.

I learn that those who were first terrified and frightened of it have since sought sanctuary on that great land mass, thinking perhaps they would have safety there, lest the inhabitants of the City of Enoch were about to fall upon the people of the world. This is not so. This is a city of love, a city of peace. We do not desire to impose our ways upon the people of the world.

Nevertheless, I am advised that many of those who stood afar off shared in wonderment when the land came up out of the sea. I am told also that the wonderment soon became anger—anger at the nobility and difference of Enoch's people, which they resented with a deep resentment. How oft the ignorance of men causes them to spend themselves in sulking instead of seeking.

I find myself pondering whether you could be among those who have repaired to that great new island, or if you are where you were before, in the land of Omner. I hope this message finds you soon.

I implore you to come and be one with us. You have been so much a friend to us; you have spoken in our behalf. There may be so little time for you to make this decision, Omner.

Enoch has prayed for this city, and he is truly a seer. He has taught us many of the things that the Lord has revealed to him, that we may learn and reason together. From the beginning Father Adam also shared many things with his children and descendants. Enoch has spoken often of his meetings with Adam, especially the one held shortly before Adam died in which many of the things that were to happen on the earth were set forth in great clarity and power.

Enoch shares much with us about those things which lie ahead and of his pleadings to God to preserve this city, for we know that the world is growing more wicked, even

59

as the people of this city are becoming more righteous. This is but one of the reasons, Omner, I wish you would hasten to join us.

While Enoch is a man of peace, he has always led his people where our enemies have come up to battle against us. His faith is great, Omner. As his scribe, I have witnessed mountains flee even according to his command, and rivers of water being turned out of their course. These things were done for a wise purpose and not merely to make display, but we have been asked not to speak at great length of such matters.

Awesome as these things were to witness, I am even more in awe of Enoch's love for all his fellowmen, yea, even those who have yet to be born. Enoch is greatly saddened by the increase in wars and bloodshed among the people of the world.

Thus, the residue of the people who fear so greatly have no need to fear Enoch. His faith and power are always employed in the service of righteous ends. Once concerned in the early days of his ministry, decades ago, about being slow of speech, Enoch has become exceedingly powerful now. Part of the power of his speech springs from the language that God has given him, for it is the pure language of Adam.

Now I must tell you, Omner, of the great and special blessing that has come to us, because the Lord Jesus Christ himself has come and dwelt among us, his people. Long have we waited for this day! The Lord himself has called us, his people, Zion because we are of one heart and one mind as we dwell in righteousness, and because there are no poor among us in this City of Holiness. My faith in him is now knowledge. How I rejoice in the goodness of God to his children!

Enoch has pled with the Lord for the preservation of the city, for the Lord has shown him in a vision how the adversary will struggle to capture the souls of all men on this planet. That the Lord loves us enough to come among us when there are so many of his creations that a man could not number them — this fills me to overflowing! Even as I write you my tears fall upon this epistle. Oh, the wondrous and endless mercies of God to his children!

There are other things approaching of which I am not privileged to speak, my friend Omner, but my love, concern, and prayers go out in your behalf. I fear lest you are almost persuaded to belief in Christ. But almost is not enough, Omner, and tomorrow is too late. One cannot become a chosen person unless he has first made *the* choice. My brother, make that choice now!

Your friend in apprehension,
Mahijah

To Mahijah, My Unfound Friend, My Anguished Greetings!

I write to you in torment of soul. For lo, after these years of desiring that I come unto you, I was at last awakened to the need to follow your counsel and to visit the City of Enoch.

Thus, laden with many troubles, anxieties, and questions, I yesterday made my way toward your city. I had not gone far in my journey when runners brought word that, at first, brought forth gales of laughter from those in my caravan, for these runners said your large city was no more in its place! That it was gone!

I determined to chide you for giving me such poor directions as soon as we were reunited; but then a chill passed through me, for these same runners had carried our communications many times for many years. They knew the way and had always returned — except for two who were so enthralled with life there that they made haste to join your throng and reside with you.

Though others along the way repeated the rumor, I persisted to the place that was the City of Enoch, and saw with my own eyes.

Of a truth, Zion is fled!

Oh, Mahijah, what has happened? Where may I find you?

At first I believed that Enoch and his people had merely departed their city for a sojourn, but now I see that the city itself is gone to sojourn I know not where.

I pondered long, wondering if your people have fled because of fear of the giants and others who conspire against you. But, alas, you have told me often and plainly of the invincibility of your city. And I myself know of the fear of all the people concerning Enoch and his people. Thus, for us, the mystery deepens and so does my sorrow.

I will now search your past epistles, some of which I have kept, for answers to my inquiry. But I am a lost man, I fear. My sorrow springs not only from the sudden sense of final separation from you, but also from stirrings and feelings within me that I have erred greatly for my own soul's sake. My pride has pressed me down for decades, even when my soul rejoiced in your words to me.

On the long journey back, for a small moment I gladdened that, perchance, Enoch's emissaries might soon come again to my household, but that hope was stilled by the realization these emissaries are no doubt gone too. Are they? Are none left?

I know not what to do with this very letter that I am preparing. To whom shall I turn? In what shall I take comfort?

I make a temporary end to this writing now, that I might forthwith search your epistles to me.

Even now my heart quickens at the fresh reading of certain of your words. Mahijah, you said that if a man lacked understanding or wisdom he might ask your God in faith, and that your God would give liberally to such an inquirer. But is that path now also no more?

If ever the once-omnipotent Omner needed answers, now is that time. This one clue you have left to me especially fills my heart and mind. I go to read it yet again. It is not much.

But could it be enough? Could it be a beginning? . . .

APPENDIX A

Synopsis of the City and People of Enoch
(See Doctrine & Covenants 107:47–49 and Moses 6,7,8)

Enoch's father, Jared, "taught Enoch in all the ways of God." Enoch was 25 years old when he was ordained under the hand of Adam, and he was 65 when Adam blessed him—the same year Enoch begat Methuselah. Enoch walked with God 365 years, and he was 430 years old when he was translated.

When he was about 65 years of age, Enoch journeyed among men, and the Spirit of God descended out of heaven and abode upon him. A voice from heaven told him to prophesy and call others to repentance, for the Lord was angry with the people, saying that "their hearts have waxed hard, and their ears are dull of hearing, and their eyes cannot see afar off." The people had gone astray, had denied the Lord, had foresworn themselves by their oaths, had sought their own counsel in the dark, had devised murder, and had not kept commandments.

Enoch humbly asked why he had found favor, for he described himself as "but a lad," as "slow of speech," and "all the people hate me." The Lord told him to go and do as commanded, and "no man shall pierce thee." He was told to "open thy mouth and it shall be filled." He was told to say to his people, "Choose ye this day to serve the Lord God." He was promised that mountains would flee before him and rivers would turn from their courses.

A saying subsequently went abroad in the land: "A seer hath the Lord raised up unto his people." In his testifying and prophesying Enoch was regarded by many as "a strange thing" and "a wild man," and at first "all men were offended because of him."

As he journeyed from the land of Cainan, by the sea east, he had a vision. Subsequently he preached and unfolded the plan of salvation, and the people "trembled, and could not stand in his presence." In recounting a vision on Mount Simeon, he taught the doctrine of the Fall and Atonement.

Enoch showed great faith and later led the people of God against their enemies. Mountains fled and rivers were actually diverted at his command. Over many years he continued to preach righteousness and built a city—the "City of Holiness—even Zion," and the Lord called this people Zion. Other nations feared Zion greatly, and there were wars and bloodshed among the residue, for "they are without affection, and they hate their own blood."

But Enoch's people came to be of one heart, one mind; they dwelt in righteousness and there were no poor among them, and the glory of the Lord was upon His people. Zion, in process of time (365 years), was taken up into God's own bosom. The saying then went forth, "Zion is fled."

APPENDIX B

Quotations from Church Leaders

SPENCER W. KIMBALL

"Again, we thank thee, O God, for another prophet who helped to set the lines straight for us — Enoch. . . . " (*Conference Report*, April 1974, p. 66.)

JOSEPH SMITH

"And now, I ask, how righteousness and truth are going to sweep the earth as with a flood? I will answer. Men and angels are to be coworkers in bringing to pass this great work, and Zion is to be prepared, even a new Jerusalem, for the elect that are to be gathered from the four quarters of the earth, and to be established an holy city. . . . " (*History of the Church*, 2:260.)

JOSEPH FIELDING SMITH

"The people of the city of Enoch, because of their integrity and faithfulness, were as pilgrims and strangers on the earth. This is due to the fact that they were living the celestial law in a telestial world, and all were of one mind, perfectly obedient to all commandments of the Lord." (*Church History and Modern Revelation*, 1953, 1:195.)

"In the day of regeneration, when all things are made new, there will be three great cities that will be holy. One will be the Jerusalem of old which shall be rebuilt according to the prophecy of Ezekiel. One will be the city of Zion, or of Enoch, which was taken from the earth when Enoch was translated and which will be restored; and the city Zion, or New Jerusalem, which is to be built by the seed of Joseph on this the American continent." (*Answers to Gospel Questions*, Deseret Book Co., 1958, 2:105.)

JOHN TAYLOR

"Thus the people in that day, had had fair warning, but only a very few paid any attention to it." (*Journal of Discourses*, 24:291.)

"But we learn that there was a Church organized about as ours may be; we learn that they went forth and preached the Gospel. . . . Enoch preached the Gospel to the people, and so did hundreds of Elders as they are doing to-day; and they gathered the people together and built up a Zion to the Lord. . . . " (*JD*, 26:34.)

"And as they gathered out from among the people, the Spirit of God was withdrawn from among the people; and they became exceedingly angry, angry at Enoch and angry at those who preached the Gospel to them." (*JD*, 26:89–90.)

WILFORD WOODRUFF

"There were not men enough in the days of Enoch who were willing to sustain that which was right; one part or other had to leave the earth; and the Lord translated Enoch and his city and took them home to Himself." (*JD*, 11:243.)

BRIGHAM YOUNG

"How long did it take Enoch to purify his people—to become holy and prepared for what we want this people to be prepared for in a very few years? It took him 365 years." (*JD*, 4:269.)

"They had not a diversity of languages, but all spoke one language; they were not trained in the various traditions in which we have been, for they received only one from Adam; they were as intimately associated as we would be living in this City two hundred years. . . . " (*JD*, 3:320.)

BRUCE R. McCONKIE

"When the perfect Zion—composed solely of the pure in heart (D.& C. 97:21)—is again established on earth, then the presence of the Lord will be felt there as his presence was found in the ancient city of that name. (Moses 7:16–19, 62–64.)" (*Mormon Doctrine*, Bookcraft, 1966, p. 361.)

"But during the nearly 700 years from the translation of Enoch to the flood of Noah, it would appear that nearly all of the faithful members of the Church were translated, for 'the Holy Ghost fell on many, and they were caught up by the powers of heaven into Zion.' (Moses 7:27.)" (Ibid., p. 804.)

FRANKLIN D. RICHARDS

"We are trying to understand the Gospel as Enoch understood it and as Christ understood it, and to do business as they did it, living in co-operation and managing our affairs in the same way, but many of us are not willing to be taught in temporal matters." (CR, April 1898, p. 18.)

JOHN A. WIDTSOE

"He [God] gave Enoch a system, known now as the Order of Enoch, or the United Order. It provided that all the citizens of Zion should work together, and that whatever was produced should be given into the Lord's storehouse, and that every man should be given from the common store according to his wants and needs. . . . The people, taught by Enoch, were able to overcome the lower feelings , and to divide all things with each other, so that all were equal." (Juvenile Instructor, 36 [1901]:364.)

"Then it was that a light was lost on the earth; and a chill crept over its surface. The sons of men moved anxiously about and peeped hither and thither. In quiet voices, such as we use when a great leader in Israel has left us, they asked, 'Where is Enoch; where is Zion, the City of Holiness?' They answered, 'Zion is fled.' " (Ibid., p. 366.)

APPENDIX C

Synopsis of the People of Nephi

The Rise (A.D. 36 to A.D. 111 — about 75 years)

The Church of Christ flourished and all people were converted. There were population growth, prosperity, and city building. There were fasting, praying, and meeting together oft to hear the word of the Lord. The people kept the commandments they had received from the Lord, and there were many miracles.

This society in this period of time is described as having —

No contentions.
No disputations.
Every man dealing justly one with another.
All things in common.
No rich, poor, bond, or free.
Peace and prosperity in the land.
A love of God in the hearts of the people.
No envyings, strifes, tumults, whoredoms, lyings, murders, or lasciviousness.
No robbers, murderers, or any "-ites."

"They were in one," "and surely there could not be a happier people."

The Decline (A.D. 111 to A.D. 245 — about 134 years.)

There was a general peace, but then a small group revolted from the church, and there began to be "Lamanites" again. The population increased, and there was exceeding prosperity. Other churches were built up and began to deny much of Christ's gospel. False prophets arose, other "-ites" (factions) appeared, and the Lamanites were once again taught to hate children of God.

Society toward the end of this period deteriorated and is described as having—

>Pride, such as in wearing costly apparel.
>Goods and substance no more in common.
>Classes and divisions among the people.
>Religious persecution.
>All manner of iniquity.
>Ostentatious church buildings.

"And the more wicked part of the people did wax strong and became exceedingly more numerous than were the people of God."

ACKNOWLEDGMENTS

Genuine appreciation is expressed to:

William James Mortimer for encouraging this enterprise;

Dallin H. Oaks, Kenneth H. Beesley, Elizabeth Haglund, Jeffrey Holland, Oscar W. McConkie, Jr., and Ellis Rasmussen for reading and sharing their suggestions;

Arthur Henry King for wise counsel concerning style and the milieu out of which Mahijah might have written;

Dean Zimmerman for providing me with quotations from General Authorities concerning the City of Zion, which should be of service to readers;

Eleanor Knowles for her careful editing;

Mahijah for lending his name (Moses 6:40);

My family for fresh forbearance;

The reader for his willingness to blow the chaff away, forgivingly, while searching for any kernels herein; and

Most of all, the Lord for such kernels as there may be.

LOOK BACK AT SODOM

A timely account
from imaginary
Sodom Scrolls

Suppose
someone had kept his impressions
of Sodom on several scrolls which
were later found. They might well
contain such things as are on
the pages to follow.

INTRODUCTION

SELDOM does a whole city or society disappear without a trace. Yet this is what happened to four towns or cities (Sodom, Gomorrah, Admah, and Zeboiim) on the plains of Siddim around 1900–2000 B.C. The best-known of these sister cities was Sodom. We have some information in the scriptures about what happened, but even less information in secular records. Significantly, Jesus Christ confirmed both the existence and the destruction of Sodom and Gomorrah during his earthly ministry.[1]

One can imagine the tremendous curiosity and excitement, therefore, that any additional information about the reasons for the destruction of this cluster of sister cities would create. *There are, of course, no "Sodom Scrolls" to supply such information. But . . .*

Suppose someone like Eliezer, Abraham's steward, had kept his cumulative impressions of Sodom on several scrolls. *Suppose* Eliezer finally gave his scrolls to Lot for review, since Lot was, after all, the one whose experience was so firsthand. *Suppose* the scrolls were left in Lot's cave in the mountains near Zoar (the one little town of the five that God spared), for Lot dwelt in a cave in the mountains up out of Zoar.[2]

---

[1]See Matthew 11:23–24; Mark 6:11; Luke 10:12; Luke 17:28–30.
[2]Genesis 19:30.

5

No doubt, *if* such scrolls were later found, they would be known as "The Sodom Scrolls," and they might well contain such things as are on the speculative pages in the fictional revisitation to follow.

These fictitious scrolls and their content do take advantage of what we know about Sodom from the scriptures and from secular sources, modest as the amount of that information is. Efforts have been made in the style to blend in relevant quotations from scriptures that obviously emerged *after* Eliezer's time; the scriptures so used either pertain to Sodom or involve timeless truths about human nature that are descriptive of things "as they are, and as they were, and as they are to come." (Both scriptural and secular sources in the scrolls are noted sequentially at the end of each scroll. Quotation marks and numbers are omitted to ease the passage of the eye. Those scriptural quotations with which Eliezer would have a personal familiarity are in quotation marks, however.)

Most importantly, the style of writing used assumes that Eliezer was a tutored steward and no ordinary helping hand around Abraham's household, for the brilliant and spiritual Abraham would need a fairly sophisticated steward. Any steward of Abraham with any kind of tenure would have had a most unusual life with many chances to see and observe many things.

The reader's understanding and patience are especially needed, however, as Eliezer becomes the eyes, ears, and voice of this fictional revisitation of Sodom using scriptures and supposings.

The Savior has warned that his second coming will occur (1) just as did the flood in Noah's time and also (2) as the raining of fire and brimstone on Sodom—as a surprise (except to the very faithful). We would do well, therefore, to ponder the lessons of the past as well as the possible parallels between our own society and the society of Sodom, *for Sodom was not just a place, but a way of life.*

6

A modern prophet, President Spencer W. Kimball, has warned us: " . . . when toleration for sin increases, the outlook is bleak and Sodom and Gomorrah days are certain to return."[3]

His predecessor, President Harold B. Lee, warned of the growing social acceptance of "that great sin of Sodom and Gomorrah . . . adultery; and beside this, the equally grievous sin of homosexuality, which seems to be gaining momentum with social acceptance in the Babylon of the world. . . . "[4]

Many today are as indecisive about the evils emerging around us — are as reluctant to renounce fully a wrong way of life — as was Lot's wife. Perhaps in this respect, as well as in the indicators of corruption of which sexual immorality is but one indicator, our present parallels are most poignant and disturbing. It was Jesus himself who said, "Remember Lot's wife."[5] Indeed we should — and remember too all that the Savior implied with those three powerful words.

While it was tragic for Lot's wife to look back, for our generation a hard look back at Sodom could save us from impending tragedies!

---

[3]"Love Versus Lust," BYU *Speeches of the Year*, January 5, 1965.

[4]*Ensign*, January 1973, p. 106.

[5]Luke 17:30–32. There is scant information about the final fate of Lot's wife. In Genesis 19:26 she is described as looking back and then becoming a pillar of salt; in Luke 17:31, Jesus' comment on her occurs in the context of his sober warning to all at his second coming that "he that is in the field, let him likewise not return back. Remember Lot's wife." Significantly, in the Old Testament, Lot's wife — before looking back — is described as looking back at Sodom from a point "behind" Lot. This is all we know, and speculation is fruitless; inferences can be drawn, but they are apt to exceed the data available. Thus Eliezer merely raises a possibility in the first scroll, but he is uncertain of the facts — beyond the essential fact of Lot's wife's destruction for disobeying a divine command to put Sodom (and all it stood for) behind her, *irrevocably!*

THE FIRST SODOM SCROLL

I, Eliezer of Damascus, write as the blessed and tutored steward of Abraham with the hope that what I have written about the follies and fate of my neighbors in Sodom will be helpful to future generations. My master's example as a record keeper in Egypt and Canaan stirred me to write also.

I, Eliezer, have now served as the steward of Abraham for many years. I was with my master when his herdsmen and the herdsmen of Lot had strife. My wise master said to Lot, "For we be brethren," and offered Lot his choice between the well-watered plain of Jordan (or the Valley of Siddim) and Canaan. I marveled at my master's generosity because the plain was exceedingly fertile, even as Eden, the garden of the Lord.

My master, Abraham, is a man of mark and sway. Often have I heard him talk of his early days in the land of the Chaldeans. Even as a young man, he knew that there was greater happiness and peace and rest for him than was to be found in his homeland. He strongly desired to be one who possessed great knowledge, and to be a great follower of righteousness, and to be a father of many nations.

He recounted how his fathers had turned from righteousness to the worship of Elkenah and other false gods.

9

He has spoken to me, too, about how the priests of Elkenah laid violence upon him, that they might slay him, and how he was rescued by the Lord. Oh, how often the human family has suffered from priestcraft!

Abraham is not only generous, but he is a gracious man. He knew that his power and priesthood could not be used except by following the principles of righteousness. It mattered not to him whether he entertained angels or strangers; he was quick to give them succor, food, and water. Never have I seen anyone who has so much knowledge of so many things and yet who is also so humble. My master understands much about the stars and the heavens and yet he is ever generous and gracious to those on the earth. His righteousness is like a light which cannot be hid, for it shines forth as naturally and regularly as the sunshine.

Lot chose the plain and pitched his tent toward Sodom, while Abraham and his people dwelt in the land of Canaan. From that time I often went to inquire after the welfare of Lot (not long before Sodom was a city in its last throes of sin and wretchedness). I kept records on scrolls, which I now abridge and complete before delivering them to Lot for his pondering and keeping; yet Lot is full of remorse, and I know not how much he will treasure these scrolls.

I will but say that I would not have believed a people could become so wicked so quickly if I had not seen it myself—including the end, which, with my master, we saw from far away early one morning as the smoke rose from what was Sodom.

I would not have wanted my family to be reared in the place and among the people where Lot's family was reared, and I rejoiced exceedingly in the wisdom of my master, Abraham, in living safely separated from Sodom. Yet Abraham pleaded for the unrighteous therein, for he cared even for the sinner. Abraham was a light to all among whom he lived, for he could be in the world without becoming like the world. I have learned from him that there can be a Zion wherever the pure in heart dwell, whether it be in the tents of one family or in a whole city.

I have set my reliance for a portion of the information contained here upon my acquaintance in Sodom, Cherazim, who when I visited the city would make known to me the growing wickedness of Sodom (sometimes recounting with a glee he did not seek to hide), which gave me a heavy heart, for Cherazim did not begin as an evil man.

I never went to Sodom after the first few years, except when I was required, and I was always exceedingly anxious to leave. This feeling was shared by the caravans that had to pass through Sodom or Gomorrah. Perhaps the reader has visited places where, when he came thither, his first feeling was an urgent desire to leave? For there was a stench about Sodom — not alone a stench which vexed the nostrils, but the heavy and oppressive feeling that comes from being immersed in sin on a large scale.

In the plain of Siddim there were four cities beside Sodom — Gomorrah, Admah, Zeboiim, and Zoar (Zoar was the smallest and also the one God later spared when Lot fervently petitioned God). These four lay near to the Dead Sea on a plain extremely fertile. Once each of the five cities had its own king, and all of these cities paid heavy tribute to a king named Chedorlaomer. But after thirteen years of such taxing and tributes, the cities rebelled. The rebellion was crushed by King Chedorlaomer, and he then took all the goods and food of Sodom and Gomorrah. Some inhabitants were also taken captive; Lot was among the captives.

Yet again did Lot's generous uncle, Abraham, make determination to help Lot. Even though Lot was held prisoner by a large victorious army, my master with but three hundred and eighteen men and brilliant stratagems followed the army well nigh to Damascus, my home, and

11

made the rescue of the prisoners. Lot was ever grateful to
my master, Abraham, for his being rescued from the As-
syrians; other captives and Lot's goods were also rescued
by Abraham's daring.

It may be that this earlier experience of being a conquered people did but hasten the hardness of the people
of Sodom, for so often the bitterness of defeat shrivels the
soul. The wise learn from their past, but the stubborn, by
their lack of understanding, err endlessly.

Yet there were many things that contributed to the
wickedness of the people of Sodom, some of which I shall
detail in subsequent scrolls. I am grateful that my master
in his learning has taught me many skills that most stewards have not the chance to learn, so I make a feeble attempt
to make a record of this people.

Fertile was the plain of Siddim, but it was not always
good for man to pass by or even dwell there. The air stank
at times because of the brimstone, which burned the nostrils and caught the throat. Some said the stench that came
and went arose from a gas under the surface of the earth.
From time to time the ground rumbled and shook, which
caused the inhabitants at first to fear, but these rumblings
grew to be the butt of many jokes; the inhabitants would
revel in warnings from the Lord, which they chose to take
as cause for laughter.

Besides, the land around Sodom was very rich, and
the regular and abundant harvests made the people forget
those hints of hell. There was even a grove in which the
inhabitants would gather annually at harvest time with
their families to feast and to celebrate. It was at times such
as these that Cherazim and others told of abominations in
the sight of the Lord. Children too young to drink wine
nevertheless drank in with their eyes scenes too wicked
to set forth on these scrolls.

Much as I was cast down by the increasing wickedness
of these cities, I had no sense of imminent disaster until

12

near the end. Only near the end did I recall afresh that my master, Abraham, once had to flee from the wickedness of his fathers, for they had turned from their righteousness and utterly refused to hearken to the Lord's voice. And I was comforted by the assurance that the righteous are always given a way to escape, if they are truly desirous of happiness, peace, and righteousness.

Nevertheless, I did marvel that sin could lay such hold upon men and that the children of men could become so entangled therein. Truly, not only do seeds and species produce after their own kind, but wickedness begets wickedness.

The sadness of Lot, who rescued his wife and daughters from Sodom just before its destruction, has since been deep and great, for his wife not only looked back toward Sodom, but may have sought to return thither. We must put our hand to the plow and not look back, for where the eyes glance back, the heart may go also.

Great indeed is the power of sin over the souls of men and women. The saddest of those whom I saw in Sodom were those few who sorrowed the sorrowing of the damned, who could no longer take happiness in their sins, but who could not truly repent either, for their hearts were not broken and their spirits were not contrite.

I make an end to this writing of the first scroll.

First Sodom Scroll (sources are listed sequentially):

Genesis 15:2

Genesis 13:5–18

Abraham, chapter 1

Genesis 18:1–8

Louis Ginzberg, *The Legends of the Jews,* vol. I, Philadelphia: The Jewish Publication Society of America, 1972, pp. 245–56

Genesis, chapter 14

1 Corinthians 10:13

Mormon 2:13–14

THE SECOND SODOM SCROLL

One of the iniquities of Sodom was pride. I have never seen pride as fierce or as unjustified as the pride of the Sodomites. They were proud of their riches; they were proud of their wealth; they were proud of their injustice toward men. They were even proud of their pride. Do not pride and wickedness go hand-in-hand? For as surely as the proud elevate themselves in their own eyes, their neighbors disappear from view. The proud not only fail to look up to God, but the proud look down on their neighbors.

The Sodomites kept no memory of the blessings they received from God. Because of their selfishness, they hated strangers with an especial hatred. A stranger was not to be helped, but to be used and abused. The very laws in Sodom were designed to harm and to worsen the state of the poor. Those who were rich were favored by the law. I was told by Cherazim that the less a man owned, the more he was obliged to render service in tribute to government. Yet though there was neglect of the poor and needy in the midst of plenty, the poor became greedy and envious themselves. The world of the wicked is a world turned upside down.

Why should those who had much goods enjoy the sport of flooding their highways so that strangers could not find, or make, their way? Why should the citizens of Sodom have been so heartless toward beasts as well as toward men? Perhaps just as kindness is contagious, so cruelty begets its own kind. Once these cities were somewhat humble after their conquest by King Chedorlaomer, but since they were compelled to be humble, their humility did not last.

Beneath their proud outward face, however, there was seen in the faces of the inhabitants of Sodom boredom and hatred of self. Because they no longer loved their God or their fellowmen, they had grown to hate life and to hate themselves. But the more fiercely they disliked life, the more fiercely did they seem to cling to it. They seemed to seek out the sensations — those things that would convince them they were still alive — and these were the most selfish vices. The Sodomites worshiped fiercely at the altar of appetite.

The weariness I saw in them was not really a weariness of life; it was a weariness of being near death, because such men were oppressed with feelings of not being alive. By service and righteousness, we are made exceedingly alive, but sin dulls us and brings us near death. So afflicted, the Sodomites sought some fresh sensation, some new sensual experience that would still assure them they were still alive; but there was a deadening of their capacity to feel with each new sin and with each new sinful sensation. Life in Sodom was much as it must have been in the days of Noah, when there likewise was much corruption and violence.

The cruelty of these cities had its links with their exceeding great wealth; the soils here seemed able to grow almost everything. Yet, the more the Sodomites had, the more they wanted; they contrived to feel envy in the midst of plenty.

Of this be assured: there was no meeting of inhabitants in which the Sodomites made sudden determination they

16

would become the most wicked city in the world. But what they once would have refused to do directly, they soon did indirectly and swiftly; they were led carefully down to hell.

Lot rightly feared early for his own sons-in-law, who were against his timely exhortations to them, because they had become so entangled in sin. Lot's wife was a woman without decision, finding it hard to make decisions without looking back on what she had decided. And she was also thoughtless; some say it was she who gave away the presence of the divine visitors in her household when she went to borrow salt from one of her neighbors. Even so, it may be unjust to expect anyone to have lived so close to Sodom and not have been infected by it.

Another sin of Sodom was idleness. Idleness brings about idolatry and increase in iniquity. There is something holy about work; even in times of plenty, it is a necessity. While work is not all of life, it nevertheless can keep us mindful of our blessings.

The very regularity of the fertility of the plain of Siddim was one of the causes of idleness, because the people needed not to labor hard in order to produce more than they needed. Thus everyone went on eating, drinking, buying, selling, planting, and building, ever seeking to satisfy their lusts for sensual satisfaction, for possessions, and for power. There was routine in the wickedness.

The Sodomites idled away their time and their talents. Thus we see how the idle are led away themselves, but also the manner in which they withhold their talents from their neighbors in need. When we do not share God's purposes, time can be a heavy curse. The idle do not rejoice and thank God for the gift of each day. Rather do they believe that time is theirs to spend solely on themselves, and they pass the needy by and notice them not, nor are they familiar with others to whom they might impart of

17

their substance. Adversity does not always produce appreciation, but affluence rarely does.

In their leisure, the Sodomites never thought to render service to others; they sought some new sensation or a new manner of an old sensation. They were turned inward on themselves. Their hardness of countenance was matched by their hardness of words, for their conversations were filthy. When I was with my master in Egypt I saw some civility and gentility, but these qualities disappeared in but one decade in Sodom.

He who reads this might ask about the leaders of Sodom. The men here, save Lot, were evil. The judges were corrupt. The city fathers had long since ceased to care about serving the people; rather they yielded to the people as the people took to their pleasures and wished no interference therein. Even as the laws multiplied what was forbidden, as in the buying and selling of things, the laws pertaining to the morals of the people diminished so as to permit anything in behavior.

There is no sin that is truly private, for ere long what is done privately will be justified and promoted publicly. A man cannot, for long, be good when the sun is high in the sky but then be bad as night comes, for such a one is divided against himself.

Moreover, a carnal and sensual soul is no friend of the poor and needy. The city fathers closed their eyes to the iniquity around them. Corruption spread wide, and whatsoever a man did was no crime.

The men of Sodom forgot to do justly and to love mercy, and their way of life was measured from bribe to bribe. They excused themselves to each other, saying that the hand of everyone took and held bribes; so should not each have his share? He who might once have been condemned of all for dishonesty became esteemed of all. The bribery was twice wicked because it gave advantage to the undeserving and it took from the deserving. And as the judges became corrupt, more and more citizens were willing to bear false witness for a fee. Cleverness was more valued than goodness, and the truth of what a man said came to matter less than his manner of speech.

But that was not the way of its beginning. A few short years ago, men who wanted more freedom simply pressed for the right to live as they pleased and to walk in their own way. Those who had asked for tolerance for themselves were later not content to let Lot or his family alone, since Lot strove to live after the manner of the Lord. What started out merely as a plea on the part of the wicked for tolerance for themselves later turned into a fierce oppression of others, and they were stirred up to anger against that which was good.

In Sodom, the wicked craved that all be wicked in the same way, even as the wretched desire that all be wretched in like manner. Men entangled with sin (taking what little pleasure they could from adultery, fornication, and homosexuality) were firm in the determination that all should do even as they did. Once each man who lived was himself and not another. Then all men became like unto one another, for sin strikes all men with the plague of sameness. Hard were the countenances of these in Sodom, and their fierceness of face could not be hid.

Lot told me many times that so filthy was the language and the profanity in the conversations of daily life in the streets and in the market that it vexed his soul every day. In my conversations with Cherazim, it was so, and in the end, I sought to avoid his company. Truly, the Sodomites could not speak peaceably one to another.

Are those who are evil always rude? Have those few who wish to live righteously always vexed those who live sinfully? I have seen the nobility of my master strive with the lukewarm, and at times the lukewarm resented his righteousness. Any man may blink as the rays of morning first touch his eyes, but some blink and then turn with

19

irritation away from all light. So it is also when some men encounter an individual illuminated by the light of truth.

The children born into these cities had no choice at all left to them. Such was the conformity in wickedness that babes could be born free, but not remain agents unto themselves. My bowels were moved within me to see innocent children not born of goodly parents, but trapped in families where fathers lived in the depths of wickedness — and the mothers likewise, for the women of Sodom became even more hard and more raucous than the men, once they gave way to wickedness. Children grew old before their time, but it could not be otherwise in families filled with fornication or in neighborhoods aggrieved by adultery. Boys learn to be men by watching their fathers, but what choice had these boys in the haven of homosexuality that was Sodom?

Of all things that were most grievous to be born was this pursuit of strange flesh, in which men seek out men; they became like a wolf pack. When they saw unwary travelers, especially men, in the street, the news of such strangers would speed through the city with great swiftness.

Even as I despaired and wondered if there were enough good people to save Sodom, my loving master Abraham pleaded with the Lord for the Sodomites. But Abraham knew that in the days of Noah only eight were righteous enough to be saved.

When Lot warned the wicked, there were those in Sodom who said they feared not death or destruction, but it was not true courage, for theirs was not the courage of those who love life but are nevertheless willing to die because of some greater cause; nay, it was willingness to die born of a disdain for life itself, a despair rooted in riotous living in a society no longer able to bear the bonds of restraint.

There once was an open theater to provide respite from

labor, but the theater became ribald and wicked. There was a time when the drama in the theater dealt with matters that were worthy of veneration and celebration. Now the drama became merely a mirror of the fornications, rapes, beatings, and murders that filled the streets and houses of the city. Out of the faces of onlookers glared the eyes of beasts in stony stares that Cherazim said at first made even Lot's sons-in-law to feel afraid. But Lot's sons-in-law soon lost their fear and mocked Lot's warnings by saying, "O thou fool! Violins, cymbals, and flutes resound in the city, and thou sayest Sodom will be destroyed!"

After some years of such life, these five cities, except for Zoar, were destroyed. A little mud sliding down a hill soon became a flood of filth, for when a people ceases in its pursuit of righteousness, it does not halt, but slithers even faster into evil.

I put an end to the second scroll.

Second Sodom Scroll (sources are listed sequentially):

Ezekiel 16:49

D&C 64:24

Ginzberg, *op. cit.*

Alma 32:13–16

Genesis 6:11–12

1 Nephi 28:21

Ginzberg, *op. cit.*

Journal of Discourses, 26:36: Brigham Young observed that Lot's "wife was a little tinctured with gentileness."

Ezekiel 16:49

Alma 1:32

Luke 17:28–29

D&C 60:13

2 Nephi 28

2 Peter 2:7–8

Isaiah 3:9

John Taylor, *The Government of God*, p. 5: "Hence it was better to destroy a few individuals, than to entail misery on many. And hence the inhabitants of the old world and of the cities of Sodom and Gomorrah were destroyed, because it was better for them to die, and thus be deprived of their agency, which they abused, than entail so much misery on their posterity, and bring ruin upon millions of unborn persons."

Parley P. Pratt, *Journal of Discourses*, 1:259: "If we were like the people before the flood, full of violence and oppressions; or if we, like the Sodomites and Canaanites, were full of all manner of lawless abominations, holding promiscuous intercourse with the other sex, stooping to a level with the brute creation, predisposing our children, by every means in our power, to be fully given to strange and unnatural lusts, appetites, and passions, would it not be a mercy to cut us off, root and branch, and thus put an end to our increase upon the earth? You will all say it would. The spirits in heaven would thank God for preventing them from being born into the world under such circumstances."

Jude 7

Ezekiel 16:49

Alma 44:5

Genesis 19:14

Ginzberg, *op. cit.*

THE THIRD SODOM SCROLL

I fear lest in my previous writings I have not done justice to my master's nephew, Lot. For Lot did strive mightily to save not only the city of Sodom, but also his own family. True it is that only he and his daughters remained alive, for his wife halted between two opinions, and his sons-in-law would not leave with him. Nevertheless, Lot had courage and was a just man.

When two divine messengers were Lot's guests, the men of the city surrounded his house. Lot did his best to shield his visitors and to protect his daughters and dissuade the rabble from evil designs. The divine visitors brought about a blindness upon the lusting men outside, who then wearied themselves trying to find the door and thereby gave a way of escape for Lot and those who would go with him.

Lot simply and plainly bade his sons-in-law, his daughters, and his wife, "Up, get you out of this place; for the Lord will destroy this city." But Lot's sons-in-law thought he mocked them and would not go.

When morning arose, the divine visitors again urged Lot to hasten and to take those who would go with him, his wife and two daughters; but Lot lingered in regret and in the end had to be led by the hand from Sodom in company with his wife and two daughters. So it was with Lot.

I have been with my master, Abraham, at times when he has had to escape or leave a land with dispatch, and I am filled with compassion for Lot in the bewilderment of those last hours. I know that it was with sadness my master, Abraham, left his father, Terah, in the land called Haran, where Terah turned again into idolatry and refused altogether to leave Haran.

It is grievous to a man when those he loves are not able to hear the truth and to respond to it, but the guilty taketh the truth to be hard, for it cutteth them to the very center. Lot in his great trial knew keenly the pressures of time were great upon him to try to persuade his loved ones in the final hours of Sodom.

When there are not enough good men to leaven a people, that people are deaf to the things of the Spirit. There was in this land of plenty a famine of righteous examples, and Lot was a solitary example. Thus did the people pattern themselves after the examples of evil, and the voice of the people did choose iniquity. Where there are enough good men to bear witness by their lives and their works that God lives (for in such cities some righteous works are done), these cities may have less mercy in the day of judgment than Sodom, which had fallen into a state of spiritual darkness such that the inhabitants could scarcely tell good from evil.

The citizens here were past feeling. They had lost their love toward God and man. As those who have known the joy of hearing music, but grow deaf and cannot discern the sounds, so only the most gross of sensations were felt by the Sodomites. How could they esteem their neighbors when they had lost their regard for themselves?

The Spirit of the Lord ceased striving with Sodom. Nevertheless, I fear that Sodom will become a watchword forever, for just as Sodom neglected its divine visitors, perhaps other wicked cities in times to come will neglect their divine emissaries and representatives.

24

The people of Sodom did evil for all to see. Their very countenances were witnesses against them.

Yea, Sodom declared its sins! Other people I have been among sometimes sought to cover their vanity and mis-doings. Nevertheless, the boldness of the sin in Sodom, the fierceness with which they pursued evil, did cause me to tremble. Sodom openly strengthened the hand of evil-doers.

Even though they had much of this world's goods, the Sodomites were never generous; even in their sensuality they were not generous, but altogether selfish. In their spiritual darkness they grew confused about what caused things to happen. They began to think that the abundance of their crops and harvests sprang from their skill, ne-glecting the God who gave them their soil and the rain that fell upon the soil, and who provided both the seeds and the sunshine that caused the seeds to sprout. The arrogance of the Sodomites was especially sinful in that they thought themselves sufficient in all things. They re-fused to give glory to God, but said haughtily that they would take the honor and the glory, even like unto him whose servants they had surely become.

Though I prayed for the Sodomites many times, my prayers were without faith, because of the great wicked-ness of Sodom. My master, Abraham, never despaired. I found the Sodomites to be without mercy, without order, without civilization, strong in their perversions, and past feeling — beyond any capacity to care for others.

At first it was the fathers who began to be immoral, for so often Satan seeks the shepherd, and then the flock comes after him. At that time among the wives and children who were still tender-hearted, I saw many hearts pierced with deep wounds. Later the women became as strong in their perversions as were the men.

The prophets have compared evil to darkness, and total darkness is always the same. Only light and illumination give variety and beauty to the earth and its people. The light had long since gone out of Sodom; sin was always in season, and the dance of life there was restless, like the waves of the sea which cannot rest. The wicked cannot rest, for wickedness wars with itself.

Now I make an end to this third Sodom Scroll, and if it so be that I am able, I will write yet another scroll. If not, even so, I am grateful that my master, Abraham, has taught me the manner of writing; though my own efforts are feeble, I rejoice in being able to leave these things. When you receive these things forgive my repetitions and the shortcomings of my words, but please do not gainsay the heaviness of my heart, out of which these words proceed, for my anguish is great concerning the destruction of Sodom and her sister cities.

Third Sodom Scroll (sources are listed sequentially):

1 Kings 18:21

2 Peter 2:7–8

Genesis 19:1–11 (King James Version)

Genesis 19:8–15 (Inspired Version)

A word of clarification concerning Lot's daughters: In the King James version of the Old Testament (Genesis 19:8), Lot is portrayed as offering to substitute his two daughters to the mob of marauding men who surrounded Lot's house, demanding that Lot deliver to the mob his two divine male visitors. Fortunately, the Prophet Joseph Smith in the Inspired Translation shows us a Lot equally determined to protect his two daughters and the divine visitors. Peter could scarcely have described Lot as a "just man" if it were otherwise.

Genesis 19:15–16

Abraham 2:5

1 Nephi 16:22

Matthew 11:23

Moroni 9:20

Revelation, chapter 11

Isaiah 3:9–10

LOOK BACK AT SODOM

Jeremiah 23:14
Ezekiel 16:99
Mormon 3:12
Moroni 9:11–20
Jacob 2:35

THE FOURTH SODOM SCROLL

I, Eliezer, desire to write yet another scroll in order to record somewhat more fully those things which pertain to the great destruction of Sodom.

As those in Sodom ripened in iniquity, my heart grew heavier, as did the hearts of those in my family, for they had known in passing some of those who dwelt in Sodom, and had even been from time to time in the dwelling of Lot. With me, my family was astonished at the seeming speed with which the Sodomites seized upon evil as a way of life. We saw together how, once the constraints of conscience are swept away, there are no barriers in the pathway of those who plunge toward the gulf of misery and endless woe. Once men cease to hearken to the counsels of God, they first say that whatsoever they do is no crime, and then they say boldly there is no crime. Truly, whatsoever a man really believeth makes determination of his deeds, and whensoever men cease to believe in God and his judgments, they cease not only to be accountable to God, but also to their fellowmen. Many such evidences were seen by me and my family in the chronicle of evil in the cities of the plain. That is why, alas, my prayers for Sodom became without faith because of their continued wickedness.

I make no pretense that I or my family knew beforehand

29

of the destruction of Sodom, but on the morn when the earth rumbled and the heavens were laced with lightning, when fire and brimstone came down like rain and when there were both the smells and sounds of great destruction, I cannot truly say that I and my family were surprised to see the destruction on the distant horizon.

Our very silence as we watched the distant fury was in sober contrast to the sights, sounds, and smells of the distant destruction. None of us spoke a word, and yet so much was said as our eyes met in grief and awe. It was so suddenly done—and so complete, except for the place known as Zoar, which God in his mercy spared—that we knew none had survived, except God had prepared a way beforehand for them as, indeed, we soon learned God had done for Lot and his very own.

What was not swallowed up was burned up, and the smoke that ascended upward as the smoke of a furnace marked the place only briefly, and at length then the winds carried even it away. And there was a stillness such as I have never heard nor felt before nor since.

Passersby and those in the trade caravans were dumbfounded when they later came to those very places where once they did barter in Sodom. Many would stop and stare at length and then depart in stony silence. Since then, the valley of Siddim has become so desolate that the trade caravans make haste around the place that was once Sodom. Would that onlooking men could learn from the past, but I fear that their wonderment was not a pondering over the mercies and judgments of God, but a brief puzzlement to be laid aside at the next stop of their journey.

Awful and mighty as was the sudden destruction that Lot witnessed firsthand once he was safely out of the city of Sodom, yet I am told that only when the multitude of evil men surrounded his place and sought to ravish Lot's divine visitors and his daughters did Lot know that the sins of Sodom had reached a point at which they were too grievous to continue in either the justice or the mercy of God.

I, Eliezer, see only as a humble steward sees, yet beyond what I have already recorded, I perceived these further things concerning Sodom.

The laughter of the licentious, which was so much a part of Sodom, is not a sign of real joy, for sensuality is sadness. The peculiar hypocrisy of the sinner is that he pretends he is happy when truly his heart is pierced with deep wounds, for wickedness never was happiness. Oh, how relentlessly the wicked seek company with others, for in departing from their God, their loneliness is an awful and a solemn loneliness.

Truly, the devil desireth that all men be made miserable like unto himself. Even the very pleasures with which he entices men to do evil are soon made empty, for the devil doth desert his own and cheateth their souls, not only out of salvation, but even out of that which he promised, for the truth is not in him.

In their fierce grasping for pleasure and wealth, the Sodomites did squeeze the joy out of everything that they did touch, for the less peace and contentment there was in their souls, the more bold did their evil become and the more overbearing their conduct. I was even led to ponder on occasion if their very rush to do iniquity did not also become a beckoning for judgment to come upon them to save them from themselves.

I seek now to make an end to my writings and to deliver these scrolls to Lot. If it so be that he may find them to be of value, he may desire to make his own a more complete record of these happenings. Yet I know his heart is exceedingly heavy, and it may be that in his remorse he cannot write of these things. Yet men must sometimes ponder the past prayerfully, if they desire to fashion a future fit to live in.

Fourth Sodom Scroll (sources are listed sequentially):
Alma 30:17
Mormon 3:12
Genesis 19:28
Isaiah 57:20–21
Mosiah 29:26–27

DEDICATION

This small volume is dedicated to the decent people of the earth everywhere who have—

- —learned from human experience what happens when badness becomes a way of life . . .
- —shunned cleverness in favor of honesty . . .
- —developed a deep and practical morality that flashes warnings to them when something, or someone, is phony or bad . . .

—been content to go unheralded, to make few demands of governments, and to abide (up to a point) the actions of others, thus making freedom possible for all, including the clever and the bad!

There were *not*, as Abraham learned, enough such individuals in Sodom (nor in the other cities on the plains of Siddim) nearly four millennia ago. Eight were rescued in the time of Noah, but finally only three from Sodom (in view of Lot's wife's fate). While the precise mathematical proportions of the critical mass of good people necessary to save a society is not known to us, it cannot be doubted that without that critical mass, societies decline rapidly and significant changes come, in one form or another, and sometimes suddenly!

The deluge in Noah's time was a disaster after which mankind began all over again. In the case of Sodom, there were three survivors, but the destruction of culture and place was total; there was no Phoenix-like reemergence; until this day one sees there only barrenness and unfertility. Where once the ungodly ate, drank, and made merry, now there is perpetual silence. But it is a special silence that shouts to those who have ears to hear!

ACKNOWLEDGMENTS

The author wishes to express appreciation to: the publisher, Wm. James Mortimer, of the Deseret Book Company, for venturing this effort, which mixes scriptures and supposings; Ellis Rasmussen for his counsel and guidance, though he and others to be thanked are in no way responsible for the material in this book; Judy Howe for help with source materials and encouragement; colleagues Dallin Oaks, Joe Christensen, Jeffrey Holland, Tony Kimball, Elizabeth Haglund, and especially Arthur Henry King, for reading the manuscript and commenting helpfully and candidly. *The Life and Works of Flavius Josephus,* as translated by William Whiston, was helpful, as were Werner Keller's *The Bible as History* and Louis Ginzberg's *The Legends of the Jews.*

Most of all, since we are obligated to "learn the lessons which the tides of history wash to our feet," the author is grateful for what has been preserved about Sodom in the scriptures, which gives us some vital data and clues.

The author is very grateful also to his family, who encouraged this writing venture, which required more discipline than any writing the author has previously attempted; even so, it may fall short of what could have emerged concerning such a relevant and deserving topic.

Gratitude is also due Eliezer, Abraham's steward, whose name I have appropriated (Genesis 15:2). Hopefully, he would at least approve the purpose of this booklet.

Finally, appreciation is extended to the reader for using his discernment between the solid, scriptural insights and my own supposings.

The sole motivation of this effort is to sharpen our sensing of the sulfurous sins about us today which threaten us, too, with deterioration and cataclysm, as more and more people worship at the altar of appetite and also seek to force the orthodoxy of relativism on others. The forces of evil now march to a louder and louder cadence called "in consequence of evils and designs which do and will exist in the hearts of conspiring men in the last days. . . . " (D&C 89:4.)